Miriam's Daughters:
Jewish Latin American Women Poets

Miriam's Daughters:
Jewish Latin American Women Poets

Bilingual Edition

edited by
Marjorie Agosín

Roberta Gordenstein
Translation Editor

Poetic License
This is a work of imagination. Any use of similes or metaphors
relating to actual people living or dead is art. It contains truths not
supported by facts.

Acknowledgments and permissions appear in the contributors
section.

Cover Design: Janice St. Marie
Book Design: Judith Rafaela
Cover Art: Liliana Wilson
Printed in the United States of America

First Edition
Library of Congress Cataloging-in-Publication Data

Miriam's daughters : Jewish Latin American women poets / edited by Marjorie Agosin;
Roberta Gordenstein, translation editor. —Bilingual ed
    p. cm.
  Includes index.
  ISBN 1-890932-13-2
  1. Spanish American poetry--Jewish authors--Translation into English. 2. Spanish
American poetry--Women authors--translation into English. 3. Spanish American
poetry--20th century--Translations into English. 4. Spanish American poetry--Jewish
authors. 5. Spanish American poetry--Women authors. 6. Spanish American poetry--20th
century. I. Agosín, Marjorie. II. Gordenstein, Roberta.

PQ7084 .M47 2000
861'.60809287'089924--dc21   00-036267

Sherman Asher Publishing
PO Box 2853
Santa Fe, NM 87504
Changing the World One Book at a Time™

DEDICATION

To Miriam and her luminous spirit, to all of the poets and translators who so generously contributed to this collection. To Roberta Gordenstein for the delicacy of her translations and to Monica Bruno for her careful reading of the manuscript. I want to especially thank Judith Asher, Julia Deisler, and Nancy Fay for their inspiration and dedication.

CONTENTS

La textura de la memoria/The Texture of Memory

Jerusalén/Jerusalem

MIRIAM

Mi hermano y yo
fuimos los testigos de Dios
sobre el desierto.
Él anotaba la vida
sobre las piedras,
yo jugaba a imaginar
el agua sobre la arena,
áspera y oscura.

Mi hermano fue el elegido,
recibió el don de todas las posibles palabras,
a Dios le gustaban sus pasos
y su aliento.

Dios se enfadó ante mi deseo
de también ser peregrina como mi pueblo,
me llenó la piel
de escamas, de peces muertos.

Entre la oscurísima oscuridad,
me quedé en un calabozo
y en la luz del jardín,
de todo desierto,
las mujeres me esperaban.
Cantaban mi nombre.

De pronto,
me di cuenta
que tan sólo mi hermano
escribía
entre las piedras los dictados de Dios,
ese Dios que me había dejado tan muda y tan sola
en aquella vasta soledad del Sinaí.

Me quedé sola
con mis mujeres
sin nombre,
sin historia,
sin Dios.
Me llamo Míriam,
canto,
otorgo palabras.

MIRIAM

My brother and I
were God's witnesses
in the desert.
He inscribed life
on the rocks,
and I played at imagining
water on the sand,
bitter and dark.

My brother was the chosen one
he received the gift of language.
His demeanor and
courage pleased God.

Angered over my desire
to be a pilgrim just like my people,
God covered my skin
with scales of dead fish.

Amid the most opaque darkness
I remained in a dungeon
and in the pure light of the garden,
of the whole desert,
the women waited for me
singing my name.

Suddenly
I realized
that only my brother
wrote
amid the rocks the dictations of God,
that God who had left me so silent and alone
in the vast solitude of the Sinai.

I stayed behind
with my women
without names,
without history,
without God.
My name is Miriam,
I sing,
I grant words.

Translated by Monica Bruno Galmozzi

Foreword
Marjorie Agosín

In the house where I grew up in Santiago de Chile I heard a Babel of whispers, songs, prayers, and languages. Spanish was my language, my mother tongue spoken in the fiestas, in the schools, and in the poetry books I loved and read out loud as poetry should be read. My maternal grandparents spoke German and Yiddish. My paternal grandparents spoke Russian and often sang to the music of a balalaika bought in a flea market at the outskirts of the city.

At school I learned Hebrew and songs in Ladino. At first I seemed to be confused with too many languages, but as the years progressed all of these languages were and continue to be a part of my inheritance as a Jew, as a poet, and as a woman. It was truly enchanting to hear and feel the depth of these many languages that embedded the narratives of the Jewish people throughout our history—an ancient people carrying their prayers and their legacy across the earth.

I must also share with you, dear reader, that not only have I carried and continue to carry the languages of my ancestors, but I have also had many names. Because I was born in the United States, my mother named me Marjorie, like the character in Howard Fast's novel *Marjorie Morningstar*. In Chile I was called Margarita; at home Magita; and at the Hebrew school, Miriam.

Just as the languages one speaks denote one's identity, one's social and historical location, the name of Miriam was especially meaningful to me as it tied me to the history of the Jewish people and the diasporas that were an essential aspect of a personal as well as universal history.

The name Miriam felt like poetry to me. It conjured ancient melodies as well as the biblical tales of fortitude and triumph and the deep quest for identity and place. Miriam, together with Moses and Aaron, led their people in search of a homeland. In this quest the story of the Jewish people is exemplified: a people in search of a home. The search for identity and belonging is also a motif for the human condition of the twentieth century—a century defined by displacements and migrations. As a young Jewish girl raised in

Catholic Chile my Hebrew name Miriam personally united me in spirit with this never ending search for belonging and identity.

This anthology, which to my knowledge is the first one of its kind to include the works of Jewish women writers of Latin America, is a part of this quest for identity. It is named *Miriam's Daughters* because Miriam must be reclaimed and reinvented as one of the most extraordinary women of the Bible—a poet in her own right, a prophet, and a singer who saved her brother Moses as well as her people. She guided the ancient Hebrews with her gifts of poetry and song; thus the history of the Exodus and consequently all diasporas are simultaneously bound to both the *Torah*—the five books of Moses that form the basis of the Hebrew Bible—and to the words of Miriam, a visionary and redeemer.

In the eloquent words of Norma Rosen, "During the arid and arduous journey toward Canaan traditional Midrash adds that it was Miriam's well as much as the manna Moses prayed for that saved the people." Rosen adds: "like the manna the water of Miriam's well could taste like anything—wine, honey, milk. Moreover it had healing powers." [1]

The poetry found in this anthology has the taste of ancient lands as well as new ones. It is rooted in the ancient city of Jerusalem, but also in the modern city of Buenos Aires. It is a poetry that is timeless and bound to a geography more concerned with a sense of history than a sense of place. Thus the voices of Miriam's daughters like Miriam herself are ancient and modern, provincial and universal.

In spite of the crucial importance of Miriam as a leader of her people she has occupied a secondary level of importance in Biblical narrative. The Midrash tells us that she was punished by God and kept confined because of her leprosy for seven days and on the seventh day Miriam prays to God soundlessly moving only her lips and says, "Am I to blame if men distort my words? Am I responsible if outlandish tales are planted among my truths?"

Miriam's words remind us of the many vicissitudes that Miriam's daughters have faced in the world occupying a marginal space in the social and political spheres of their nations. And in spite of all these trials Miriam and her daughters have persisted and endured. In

Norma Rosen's words "...Both the old legends and ours must say the same. She both died and she persisted. She was ground down and then she continued. She gave up and she endured." [2]

The voices of this anthology have also endured. As a collection, it attempts to incorporate the voices of a literary tradition that has been growing in the Americas and Europe since the 1970s. Much of the American tradition—particularly in the United States—is and has been centered around the emigrant/immigrant experience. The Jewish literary tradition in Latin America, and especially that of Jewish women, has an interesting parallel and shared history with immigrant literature of the United States. The birth of multiculturalism in the 1970s and the existence of many minority groups side by side since then has made it possible for this literature to take shape and grow. At the same time, the increased awareness of national identities and the desire to return to one's roots has been a major part of the multicultural movement and is reflected in this body of work. The focus on Jewish Latin America comes from a deep necessity to give voice to an ignored identity and to inscribe that voice in a collective history of the Americas. The women in this anthology have made the significant statement that the personal is also historical.

The history of the Jews in Latin America can perhaps be dated to the arrival of Christopher Columbus in the New World in 1492 and traced to the era when the Spanish and Portuguese colonized the Americas in search of wealth and freedom. Yet Jewish historiography in Latin America has been a silenced one, in part due to the fact that Jews comprise only one percent of the population of the twenty-one Latin American republics. Although they have integrated into Latin American society, Jews have always been strangers and diasporic beings who in certain moments of history have been persecuted by government officials and at other moments have been leaders and voices in those same governments.

Nevertheless, the presence of Jewish culture has created an intellectual, artistic, and alternative space within the Latin American landscape. Jewish women writers of Latin America are beginning to be known in many countries outside of their regions, having achieved recognition vis-à-vis Latin American authors in the 1970s who immersed themselves in questions of identity, genealogies, and the transformations of memory. Authors such as Margo Glanz of

Mexico with her book *Genealogies,* as well as Argentina's Alicia Steimberg, who wrote *Musicians and Watchmakers,* are two outstanding examples of women who seek the origins of their identity as Latin American Jews. The anthropological and literary work of Teresa Pozecanski also recollects the history of the first Jews to arrive in Uruguay. Each of these poets has connected her Jewish origins to her Latin American and national identity.

The extraordinary literary outpouring of these and many other women who have begun to explore their Jewish origins is revisiting and redefining the concept of genealogy. The issue of an entire generation born of immigrants, many of them Holocaust survivors, contributes to this grand and universal exploration. *Miriam's Daughters* responds to this vital tradition of Jewish women writers of Latin America. It brings together women who raise questions in their poetry about the diasporic experience and the experience of post-Holocaust generations who have been moved and touched by the experience of their ancestors and their own distinctive roles as bearers of memory.

It is in this spirit and vision of diasporic culture, focused on memory and remembrance, that this anthology is born. It is the first collection to date in any language that brings together these voices of such high lyrical caliber.

Miriam's Daughters responds not only to the Jewish experience, but to the images that create and imagine what it means to be part of the Wandering Jewish tradition with its western and universal implications. This universal condition of exile has been one of the dominant themes of the twentieth century, and these poems embrace the many meanings of exile and of being a woman. The voices of these poets interact between the past and the future, between the dead and the living.

Divided by theme, the collection consists of four sections: *Genealogies, Illuminations, Textures of Memory,* and *Jerusalem.* The poems selected for each section correspond to an essential condition of these wandering and searching poets. The anthology begins with a deep exploration of the meanings of origins and ancestry, as well as genealogy and the complex lineage of Jews throughout history. Alina

Wechsler, an Argentine poet living in Spain, begins the series on origin with her elegiac poem "A Child is Born," a work that resonates with biblical and modern meanings. The female voice observes the pain and exile that has characterized the Jewish people: "Pain is your mark. And mine."

The subsequent poem by the actress and poet Shlomit Baytelman, born in Israel and raised in Chile, makes us participants in her obsession over identity. She confronts the issue of being and not being part of a new world of strangers, where places connote meeting and forgetting: "They brought me to South America, the land where they were born, of foreign parents. So does history turn and come back."

If the history of this poetry is dominated by a century of migration, transculturation, and exile, by remembering the past and engaging in the present, the section *Illuminations* establishes the presence of what is permanent and ambiguous about the alchemy and numerology of an unpronounceable name of God. This section is dedicated to the mystical side of Judaism, to the Kabbala, to the *Zohar,* or the book of splendors and the figures, which have formed the vibrant imaginary Jew. Some of the poems address the kabbalist rabbi based on true characters such as Benjamín de Tudela who guarded the words and sacred books of God, while others speak of the Golems that roam cities of memory and cities of myth. While the poetic treatment of genealogies is marked by a search for uncertain and disquiet origins, the poems of *Illuminations* treat a religious and mystical poetry in search of the name of God and the revelations of his imminence, magic, and divinity.

The presence of this luminosity seems united to the act of writing and to the mystery of the alphabet and creation. Rosita Kalina of Costa Rica tells us: "Next they invented alphabets./ From one the aleph was born...." If the aleph is the beginning of the Hebrew alphabet, it also represents the origin of enchantments, omens, and mysteries. The poetry of Angelina Muñiz Huberman of Mexico retains a rhythm anchored in the ineffable "unpronounceable word without echo in the sanctuary." All the authors engage in a union of history and mythology as they relate to the sacred books of Judaism.

With these illuminations that play with the lips of God and with his unsaid name, we find mystical poems that resemble Santa Teresa de Avila or the verses of Saint John of the Cross, linking the poetry of these contemporary women with a permanent ancestral heritage: that of the female Spanish Jew, a historical and literary figure that has resurfaced in the last decade.

The third section of the anthology brings us directly to the experiences of the twentieth century and to what is often called the post-Holocaust memory. Forming the base of *Acts of Memory* is the Holocaust, which not only terminated the lives of six million Jews, but eradicated the entire Jewish culture of several European nations. Although it is not a literary motif, the Holocaust continues to be a central metaphor for these poets who, as writers, become witnesses to that sinister epoch in history. Rosita Kalina writes a moving poem dedicated to Anne Frank in which the poet herself joins in a dialogue with God in order to revindicate and rememorialize Anne's life: "Lord, make me worthy of this number./ Remember, like yesterday, what burning arrow/ passes over the earth./ My wrathful cross nails itself into your enigmas." If the presence of the Holocaust becomes a continuing metaphor for these poets, the poem of Nora Strejilevich, *When They Robbed Me of My Name*, which ends this section, makes us aware that the Latin American military dictatorships were equally horrifying to the Jews:

> I was one out of a hundred, out of thousands
> and I was no one.
> Deprived of gesture, gaze and voice
> my face was reduced to the letters, NN.

It is evident in this section that the memory of the Holocaust in a post-Holocaust generation is very active and vital. Its presence in these poems is both moving and complex. Myriam Moscona imagines the garden of Auschwitz and writes: "I dreamed of Auschwitz,/ horses, stokers, executioners and buffoons." At once this poem evokes an image that is both familiar and paralyzing as it stands before the Machiavellian presence of a calculated death and rationally premeditated death. Marta Kornblith of Peru returns to ask about the presence of poetry as a way to reclaim fear or to speak of the unnamed: "That is why we dedicate our books to the dead./ Because we hold the vain belief/ that they listen to us."

In these poems there is a sense of the miraculous in survival. The memory of the Holocaust, which in its retelling evokes images of lost objects, of golden teeth, of scorched hair and the ever-present smoke, proves how its power will live on in future generations that also participate in acts of memory. These poets, who articulate the memories of the disappeared, the silenced, and the unnamed in the mass graves, continue to seek expression for this almost unspeakable historical moment.

Alejandra Pizarnik, the extraordinary Argentine poet, appears in the anthology at the apex of a universe overridden with black angels where death is present and precise in its comings and goings. She recovers for us a large part of this death imagery by converting it into curtains of smoke, clouded bodies that ask if there is still sun outside because they cannot see even themselves amidst the smoke. In another verse she alludes to the inability to truly exist when there is an absence of identity. These poems evoke a phantom world of bones and ashes as the poet ceremoniously recollects them, gathers them and names them in an attempt to bring back the dead and the living.

The memory of an entire people and its genocide lives on in the words and lives of those who remember and give it a name. The poetry of Jocelyn Goldberg is dedicated to Luba, her grandmother who survived the Holocaust. These tender poems, brief and ephemeral, are marked by the presence of memory as if memory creates a constant portrait:

> *Luba*
> *conversation*
> *along daily corridors*
>
> *Root*
>
> *Memory that I am.*

From the memory of Auschwitz and its dead garden of horrors to the voices of the survivors gathered on the lips of the poets, the memory of the Holocaust is also the memory of the living.

Miriam's Daughters concludes with a final song dedicated to the city of Jerusalem, a city that is loved and sacred to the three major Western religions, making it a city that is also besieged and disputed. The poets in this section sing to Jerusalem and their transparent voices evoke the water and eternal fountain of Miriam, the figure at the center of this collection. Miriam is a woman who embraces creativity, and is beloved by her people and heard by all women. The sacred city of Jerusalem, a city of wars and peace, a city of beggars and King David, is now the city of these women who laud its presence. Luisa Futuransky jubilantly celebrates it in "Jerusalem, a Whirling Glass." Olga Weisz Klein, who was raised in Israel and lives in Chile, takes the voice of her homeland, of history and of Israel itself, when she writes:

> *Jerusalem, I am a pilgrim*
> *the crying soldier at the wall*
> *the blood of the fallen*
> *the cry of the wounded.*
> *I am that which fed our people and*
> *your soul, your conscience and your destiny.*

Questions of origins, exile, permanence and the diasporic condition are not only important to Jews but to humans of all origins. This varied collection represents the many faces of exile and homeland. The presences and absences revealed to us in this fountain of voices are ultimately transparent like the fountain and words of Miriam herself, a prophet, musician, and gatherer of people and words.

The reader of *Miriam's Daughters* will be able to experience as well as participate in the rich and hybrid tradition found in these poems— poems that conjure the ancient images of Mea Shearim, kabbalistic rabbis, and Anne Frank. It is a poetry written in Spanish, but is also a poetry rooted in a millennial memory of exile, dispersion, as well as quest for belonging. It is a poetry that articulates and carries the memories of ancient sages, as well as the historical experience of a people united through verses that are filled with sorrows and joys and the longings to belong. In *Miriam's Daughters* the universal quest to become a part of this world and reclaim a voice is exemplified with great beauty and fortitude by these poets at home in the Spanish and Portuguese languages and in the language of history.

[1] *Biblical Women Unbound*, Norma Rosen (Jewish Publication Society, 1996).
[2] Ibid.

Genealogías/Genealogies

UN NIÑO NACE

Allí, en la Tierra Prometida,
a causa de migraciones de las aves parlantes,
un niño nace.
Lejos aún del ruido de metrallas,
de los hombres que penan su arrogancia,
de tu vientre nuevo, nace.
¿Qué tierras andará,
qué laberintos dejará su marca?
Allí, en la Tierra Prometida,
donde los Siglos declaran su peso,
a causa de migraciones de las aves parlantes,
tu hijo nace.
Sueña José,
que para él no sueñe vacas flacas
porque de tu vientre henchido
de esperanza y desgarro,
tu niño nace.

La vida vuelve a erguirse
en torno al rito
¿Quién dice que a la mujer algo le falta,
quién lo dice aún, me pregunto,
al asirte la mano de tu desgarradura ancestral
en pleno Siglo Veinte?
El dolor que desde tus infiernos
lanzas
hacia las estrellas.
Para el Júbilo, mañana sonarán las trompetas
y dulces melodías orientales
acompañarán tus sueños.
El dolor es tu marca. Y la mía.
Aunque luego lo olvidemos.

ELINA WECHSLER

A CHILD IS BORN

There, in the Promised Land,
because of migrations of chattering birds,
a child is born.
Far still from the noise of machine guns,
from the men who suffer their arrogance,
from your new womb, he is born.
What lands will he traverse,
in what labyrinths will leave his mark?
There, in the Promised Land,
where the Centuries declare their weight,
because of the migrations of chattering birds,
your child is born.
Joseph dreams,
let Joseph not dream lean cows for him
because from your womb
swollen from hope and grief,
your child is born.

Life rises up again
around the ritual
Who says that woman lacks something,
who still claims that, I wonder,
upon seizing your hand in your ancestral rending
at the height of the Twentieth Century?
The pain that from your hell
you pitch
starward.
Joyously, tomorrow the trumpets shall sound
and sweet melodies of the Orient
will accompany your dreams.
Pain is your mark. And mine.
Although later we forget it.

Translated by Darrell Lockhart

ME LLAMO SHLOMIT

Me llamo Shlomit. Nací en Afula, en la Galilea.
Me contaban que, al mismo tiempo, en el mismo lugar
nació un niño árabe.
Viví en Ramoth Menashé, el Kibutz donde mis padres
sacaban piedras todavía.
Me trajeron a la América del Sur, la tierra
donde ellos habían nacido de padres extranjeros.
Así la historia vuelve y se va; gira hacia
uno y otro lado; nos lleva sobre aguas torrentosas.
Náufragos anclando en Buenos Aires, para tomar el
interminable tren transandino calado por el frío
del carro de 2a.
Y aquí me encuentro en Santiago
explicando este nombre que tiene algo de Biblia y piedra
y calor del aire del desierto y una música.

SCHLOMIT BAYTELMAN

MY NAME IS SHLOMIT

My name is Shlomit. I was born in Afula, in Galilee.
I'm told that an Arab child
was born at the same time, in the same place.
I lived in Ramoth Menashé, the Kibbutz where my parents
are still pulling stones from the ground.
They brought me to South America, the land
where they were born, of foreign parents.
So does history turn and come back; it winds around
one and another side; it carries us over rushing waters.
Shipwreck anchored in Buenos Aires, to catch the
interminable train across the Andes, chilled to the bone
in the second-class, coach car.
And here I find myself in Santiago
explaining this name that has a bit of the Bible and stone
and the heat of the desert air and music.

Translated by Elizabeth Horan

SE DIBUJA UN PAISAJE DE RETORNO

Se dibuja un paisaje de retorno
Voces
Idioma nacional   la música
de las esferas
Quizá por estar en el aire
Por estar
   en un vuelo
Por estar
   en tránsito de retorno
Tránsito
   Sinagoga del tránsito
El catálogo minucioso de la tribu
   Ceuta
     Tánger
       Orán
La breve cárcel
las ajorcas
el mito del Moro y las canciones
La intersección: siete lenguas
Casablanca:
   el final de una historia que no se
   cuenta ni de contar
Orán:
   el nombre que circuncidó la dicha
     incircuncidable
Sin la a no hay concierto
   Solo habrá
Tránsito
Paisaje de retorno
El ángel viene a transverberarte un pulmón adicto
   a la tradición literaria
     No solo
La tradición encalada de un convento
Confundís un cuartel con un convento
     igual
que a tu casa de
     hija
       madre
        abuela

A SCENE OF RETURN IS SKETCHED

A landscape of return is sketched
Voices
National language   music
of the spheres
Perhaps because of being in the air
Because of being
            in flight
Because of being
            in transit
Transit
            Synagogue of Transit
The detailed catalogue of the tribe
            Ceuta
                  Tangiers
                        Oran
The fleeting prison
the bangles
the myth of the Moor and the old songs
The intersection: seven languages
Casablanca:
            the end of a tale that is never told
                  but counts
Oran:
            the name that circumcises that which is said to be
                  uncircumcisable
Without the A there is no concert
            just Solos
Transit
Scene of return
The angel comes to transfix a lung addicted
            to the literary tradition
                  not alone
The whitewashed tradition of a convent
You confuse a headquarters with a convent
            the same
as your
            daughter's
            mother's
            grandmother's house

Ortopedia
        deseada
El espejo
Tu sino en un papel
Un convento, quiere
Un encierro blanco en el cual
ser
        atravesada
        transverbereda
        maridada con
Padre y maestro
Lirófobo
        cántame
Dime
        Hazme
                Fúndame
                        Cúbreme
El que teme la lira
                la música de las esferas
No llegará
Llegada
Panorámica oblicua
Padre
        Madre
Tío
        Tía
¿Qué hago aquí?
Huyo a una fiesta
Fiesta
        ¡pronto!
                Fiesta
Recuérdenme
        Soy yo
                Estoy aquí
No es posible sin dioses una fiesta
Un tal...
        Un tal...
Mesié Fifí!
        Mesié Fifí!
Oh llama de amor
El rey se muere
El rey ha muerto
Viva el rey

Orthopedia
      wanted
The mirror
Your fate on a piece of paper
A convent, wants
A white enclosure in which
to be
      traversed
      transfixed
      wedded to
Father and master
You, who fears the lyre
      sing to me
          tell me
              make me
                  endow me
                     cover me

He who fears the lyre
      the music of the spheres
Won't arrive
Arrival
Slanting view
Father
      Mother
Uncle
      Aunt
What am I doing here?
I run away to a party
A party
      quickly!
          A party
Remember me
      It's me
          I'm here
There is no party without gods
A fellow called...
      A fellow called...
Mesié Fifí!
      Mesié Fifí!
O flame of love
The king dies
The king has died
Long live the king

Translated by Mercedes Roffé

LA REFUGIADA

Lucy Lipschutz, Lucy Lipschutz,
eras refugiada europea en Argentina.
Teníamos menos de diez años de edad
e íbamos a la misma escuela.
Te recuerdo alta, delgada, de ojos lánguidos
y largas trenzas de pelo oscuro.

Hablabas tu segunda lengua
cuidadosamente y con acento.
Nunca me contaste ni te pregunté
de dónde venías ni cómo llegaste.

Para mí la guerra mundial no era más
que los titulares del diario y
los noticieros de la radio
que mis padres devoraban.

Yo vivía mi vida plácida
de niña protegida.
No entendía nada, no sabía que no entendía
ni que hubiese algo para entender.

Ahora, tantísimos años y un país después,
yo, que también hablo mi segunda lengua
cuidadosamente y con acento
quisiera volver a verte, Lucy Lipschutz,
para pedirte disculpas por lo que te hicieron
y por lo que nunca hice por ti.

THE GIRL REFUGEE

Lucy Lipschutz, Lucy Lipschutz,
you were a European refugee in Argentina.
We were less than ten years old
and attended the same school.
I remember you tall, slender, with listless eyes
and long, dark braids.

You spoke your second language
carefully and with an accent.
You never told me and I never asked
where you came from, how you got here.

For me the World War was nothing more
than the newspaper headlines
and radio news programs
that my parents devoured.

I lived the cozy life
of a protected little girl.
I didn't understand anything, I didn't know that I didn't understand
or if there was anything to understand.

Now, so many years and a country later,
I, who also speak my second language
carefully and with an accent,
want to see you again, Lucy Lipschutz,
to ask your forgiveness for what they did to you
and for what I never did for you.

Translated by Celeste Kostopulos-Cooperman

TODOS LOS MESES

Todos los meses
un hijo que no tuve
se me deshace en sangres
y me disuelve entrañas.
En un parto pequeño,
una muerte modesta,
la sangre, la semilla,
los tejidos, la sangre.
Latiendo en el cerebro
del año dos mil cinco
no podrás ver los ojos
de cuatrocientos niños.
Una guerra siniestra,
una muerte modesta,
no podrás ver el rostro
de cuatrocientos niños.

TERESA PORZECANSKI

EVERY MONTH

Every month
a child I did not bear
melts away from me in torrents of blood
and dissolves my core.
In a miniature labor
a modest death
blood, seed,
tissues, blood.
Beating in the brain
of the year two thousand five
you will not be able to see the eyes
of four hundred children.
A sinister war,
a modest death,
you will not be able to see the faces
of four hundred children.

Translated by Roberta Gordenstein

HIJA PRÓDIGA

Como hija pródiga he regresado a mis recuerdos:
he rebuscado los sencillos: los inalterados.

Dejé atrás ese sentir inconforme,
ese camino de brújula sin norte,
ese plato vacío de hambre insatisfecha.

Pedí un alto en el sollozo,
una pausa en el ocaso,
un olvido de lo cercano,
por una presencia de lo lejano.

¿Cómo retomar la historia quebrantada,
el punto escapado de la aguja?
Si ya no está mi padre para
contarme cuentos prodigiosos,
ni mi madre para enhebrar mi tejido.

Cuando he querido retornar, como hija pródiga,
el umbral traspasado era depósito de cenizas,
las columnas no sustentaban techo alguno
y puertas y ventanas habían escapado
hacia cielos de escombros de guerra perdida.

Ser hija pródiga no era no traer nada
sino ante el hogar devastado
ni siquiera hallar un rescoldo,
una piedra aún caliente,
un vaho, un retoño, una espiga.

Hundir las manos en las cenizas
y como antigua sacerdotisa
esparcirlas sobre mi cabeza,
y rasgar mis vestiduras
y dejar resbalar, por primera vez,
el llanto recuperado, lágrima a lágrima,
río tranquilo, trasparente cordón umbilical,
de la hija pródiga que ha encontrado al retornar
el espacio habitado de sus muertos amados.

ANGELINA MUÑIZ HUBERMAN

PRODIGAL DAUGHTER

As a prodigal daughter I have gone back to my memories:
I have sought after the simple ones: the unaltered ones.

I have left behind that old inconformity
that path with a compass that marked no northern point
that empty plate of unsatisfied hunger.

I asked for a halt to the sobs,
a pause in the twilight,
an oblivion for that which is so near,
a presence of that which is so far.

How to recapture the broken story,
how to grab the stitch that escaped the needle?
My father is no longer here,
he who could tell me prodigious stories
My mother is not here either,
she who could always thread again my weaving.

When I have wanted to go back as a prodigal daughter
the crossed threshold was a well of ashes,
the columns didn't hold a roof
and the doors and windows had escaped
toward skies of debris from lost wars.

To be a prodigal daughter
did not mean to bring nothing
but before the devastated home
not to find even an ember,
a stone still warm,
a breath, a bud, a sprig.

To sink my hands in ashes
and as an ancient priestess
to throw them on my head
and tear my robes
To let, for the first time,
recovered tears roll down, one by one,
oh peaceful river, clear umbilical cord
of the prodigal daughter who has found back at home
the space inhabited by her beloved dead.

Translated by Aurora Camacho

ESA MUJER DE LAS CRUZADAS,

mi madre
que me vestía en ropas usadas de dogmas
trozos de zapallos sobre el sink de la cocina
            "podríamos haber salvado al niño
            al mundo
            a los Rosenbergs."

La leche se enfurece en la olla
golpea por los lados
le sale una espesa espuma

Mamá, tu también tenías rabia
pasabas repartiendo peticiones
golpeando las puertas vacías

Mientras los pensionistas pasaban aire y patatas
tu pasabas peticiones
boicoteabas a Bayers
        decías recuerda al hombre olvidado
        los 10 de Hollywood
        los muchachos de Scottsboro
        benditos sean, amen.

Parada en Times Square
eras mi árbol
una placa brotando de sus manos

Temblando, yo descansaba mi cabeza en tu cadera
hasta que me decias
mira, lo hacemos por los niños

Bajo tu árido cartel que reposaba sobre la pared
me protegias de la lluvia y me criabas en la sombra de la Causa

Translated into Spanish by Marjorie Agosín

DIANA ANHALT

THAT JEWISH CRUSADER,

my mother,
who dressed me in hand-me-down dogma,
shreds cabbage over the kitchen sink:
>"We could have saved the child,
>saved the world,
>saved the Rosenbergs."

Milk rages in its saucepan,
knocks against its sides,
foams up around the lid.

Mother, you raged too,
knocking your picket sign
against barred doors.

While the boarders passed air and potatoes
you passed petitions,
boycotted Bayer's, prayed:
>*Remember the Forgotten Man,*
>*The Hollywood 10,*
>*The Scottsboro Boys*
>*Blessed-be-they-amen.*

Standing in Times Square,
you were my tree,
a placard sprouting from your upraised arm.

Shivering, I'd rest my head against your hip
until you'd scoop me up and cry:
"Look! We do it for our children."

Under your down-turned picket sign propped up against a wall,
you sheltered me from rain and raised me in the shadow of the Cause.

LILITH, PRIMERA COMPAÑERA DE ADÁN

Una suerte de fijeza al árbol genealógico,
a los muertos,
invita en ocasiones a perderse
en la Boca de los Siglos.
Como un sapo irreverente a la orilla del río,
como el imán que me lleva a tu cuerpo y a tu oído.
Si Eva no fue la primera
qué desorden de la letra,
qué traspié en el poder del jeroglífico.
Una suerte de fijeza,
Gioconda mirando al infinito.
Una madre será por todas las madres,
Eva robará las tentaciones de Lilith,
las suyas,
por un pequeño error bíblico.

ELINA WECHSLER

LILITH, ADAM'S FIRST COMPANION

A sort of attachment to the family tree,
to the dead,
invites you occasionally to lose yourself
in the Mouth of Centuries.
Like the irreverent toad on the river bank,
like the magnet that draws me to your body and to your ear.
If Eve was not the first,
what confusion of the word,
what a blunder in the power of the hieroglyphic.
A sort of attachment,
Gioconda gazing into infinity.
A mother for all mothers,
Eve shall steal the temptations of Lilith,
her own,
because of a small biblical error.

Translated by Darrell Lockhart

COINCIDENCIA

A veces me da miedo
ser hija de una genealogía
tan ilustre.
Primer hombre, la sangre
que poseyó una piedra, un desierto lleno de ira,
un nombre innombrable y
una circulación de raíces se arman
en este cuerpo humano
que habito.

A veces me da miedo
haber nacido
el día en que nació la mano múltiple
que está detrás del espectral Macbeth
y la armadura del sueño de Alonso Quijano,
con su afiebrado y hético palimpsesto,
el de las curiosidades derramadas.
Los tres llevamos el mismo signo
                    (no el mismo destino)
y la pluma sedienta de papel, aderezo
de sangre donde se confunden el alimento y
los ausentes.

A veces me dan miedo
las sacralidades vacilantes,
los muertos que amenazan con su aura de
ceniza,
el día goteando aire blanco, cosas, ternuras.
A solas
guardo el alimento de la fragua,
las brújulas desorbitadas,
la sal espesa y lenta de las palabras, la lluvia que
arde
y que empapa de amores furiosos la piel.

AIDA GELBTRUNK

COINCIDENCE

Sometimes it frightens me
to be the daughter of so illustrious
a genealogy.
The first man, the blood
a stone possessed, a desert filled with wrath,
an unpronounceable name and
a circulation of roots are joined together
in this human body
I inhabit.

Sometimes it frightens me
to have been born
on the day when the multiple hand was born
that is behind the spectral Macbeth
and the fashioning of Alonso Quijano's dream,
with his feverish and consumptive palimpsest,
he of the overflowing curiosities.
The three of us carry the same sign
                    (not the same destiny)
and the pen thirsty for paper, seasoning
of blood where food and the absent ones
are mixed together.

Sometimes I fear
the vacillating sacred objects
the dead who threaten with their ashen aura,
the day dripping empty air, things, tendernesses.
Alone
I save the food from the forge,
the compasses out of proportion,
the thick and slow salt of the words, the rain that
burns
and soaks the skin with furious loves.

Translated by Roberta Gordenstein

SOBREVIVENCIAS

Soy hija
de tantos lugares
dejados atrás:
Silivri, Turquía
Goworowo, Polonia
Linka, Byelourusia
La Habana, Cuba
Kibbutz Gash, Israel
141-41 en la calle 85
Jamaica, Nueva York,
apartamento esquina del sexto piso
al lado del niño de la India
que sacó la cabeza de la ventana
para cazar una mariposa
y murió soltando un río
de recuerdos de sus oídos.

Las únicas cosas
que he guardado del viaje
son mi español
de demasiados acentos
mi temperamento cruel
mi miedo a los fantasmas judíos
y mi total incapacidad
de perder en el amor.

RUTH BEHAR

SURVIVALS

I am a child
of so many places
left behind:
Siliviri, Turkey
Goworowo, Poland
Linka, Byelorussia
Havana, Cuba
Kibbutz Gash, Israel
141-41 85th Street,
Jamaica, New York,
sixth floor corner apartment
next door to a boy from India
who leaned out the window
to catch a butterfly
and died oozing a stream
of memories from his ears.

The only things
I have retained from the journey
are my Spanish
of too many accents
a bad temper
fear of Jewish ghosts
and an inability
to lose in love.

Translated by Ruth Behar

SOY DE LA TRIBU DE YEHUDÁ

Soy de la tribu de Yehudá.
La de mis abuelos y bisabuelos.
La de Salomón, de Jesús y Einstein.
Por no citar a Freud,
cuyo valioso secreto cabalístico
saltó a la silla del Terapeuta.
No perdono los miles de holocaustos
que en nombre de fementidas verdades
se urdieron contra mi pueblo,
contra otros pueblos antiquísimos,
más sabios que la ley del blanco.
Me horroriza el hombre integrado
a religiosas guerras.
Que somos uno en la inmensa nave
madre tierra, quien nos transporta
a ilimitadas dimensiones.
Que todos respiramos un mismo destino.
Soy universal. Simplemente una mujer
que se atreve a soñar con una hermandad
sin credos, sin aisladas divinidades,
sin escogencias.
Precisamente por mi origen,
comprendo la tristeza de otros
venidos a menos por color o ángulo
de los ojos.
!Que venga la era del hombre,
maravilloso ser que puebla la existencia!
En él veo el único, irrepetible,
mi orgullo de ser mujer.
También amo al animal y a las plantas
que vivifican mis soledades.
Soy judía. Tersa hasta la caricia.
Amorosa hasta el éxtasis.

ROSITA KALINA

I AM OF THE TRIBE OF YEHUDA

I am of the tribe of Yehuda
The one of my grandparents and great-grandparents.
The tribe of Solomon, of Jesus and Einstein.
Not to mention Freud,
whose valuable cabalistic secret
jumped to the therapist's chair.
I do not forgive the thousands of holocausts
that in the name of treacherous truths
were plotted against my people,
against other ancient peoples,
wiser than the white man's law.
I am horrified by the man who is integrated
with religious wars.
We are one in the inmense ship
mother Earth, that transports us
to unlimited dimensions.
We all breathe the same destiny.
I am universal. Simply a woman
who dares to dream about a brotherhood
without creeds, without isolated divinities,
without discriminating.
Precisely because of my origin,
I understand the sadness of others
brought down because of the color or angle
of their eyes.
Let the era of man come,
marvelous being that populates existence!
In him I see the only, inimitable,
my pride of being a woman.
I also love the animals and plants
that vivify my loneliness.
I am Jewish. Smooth to caress.
Loving unto rapture.

Translated by Maria Xirinachs

SEGUNDO RETRATO

Soy el silbido de la noche
que huye ante el ave cazadora
en una barca encallada

Una esfera que descansa
en un árbol de Magritte
y acude salvaje
al llamado de su amo
cuando huele la lluvia en las axilas

Un movimiento fugaz
antes de la siesta
cuando la telaraña
teje las miradas entre la piel

Soy un pirata de abordajes continuos
que huele el pan casero
y los profana con un alarido
hasta devorar los pecados
—manzana quieta con los colores en el cuerpo—

Un frágil cordón
que flota sin sobresaltos
o una pantera que asusta al desprevenido
y los devora en pequeñas vibraciones
para gozar del ritual
cada vez que su sangre es sacrificio

Soy la sobreviviente de alabanzas y exterminios
en una aldea de Lituania
que aún arde en la memoria

MANUELA FINGUERET

SECOND PORTRAIT

I am the whistling of night
that flees before the bird of prey
in a boat run aground

A sphere that rests
in a tree by Magritte
and savagely rushes in
at the call of its master
when he smells rain in his armpits

A fleeting movement
before the siesta
when the cobweb
weaves glances into the skin

I am a pirate of constant boardings
who smells homemade bread
and profanes it with a scream
until the sins are devoured
—peaceful apple with colors on its body—

a fragile cord
that floats without fright
or a panther that frightens the unprepared
and devours him in small vibrations
to enjoy the ritual
each time his blood is a sacrifice

I am the survivor of prayers and exterminations
in a Lithuanian village
that still burns in memory

Una maga púrpura
a la que recitan salmos
y no desea despertarse
porque es tan blanca la mañana
y breve el encantamiento
que un resplandor la agita

Soy una flecha en el universo
que tiembla cuando un hijo crece
y cuyo destino
es un manto dorado de hojas secas
en un punto ascendente de la vía láctea.

A purple enchantress
to whom they recite psalms
and who does not wish to awaken
because morning is so white
and enchantment so brief
that a flash of light can stir her

I am an arrow in the universe
that trembles when a child grows
and whose destiny
is a golden mantle of dry leaves
in an ascendant point of the Milky Way.

Translated by Roberta Gordenstein

PESADILLA

Otra vez el mismo sueño.
Estoy en la calle, en una ciudad desconocida.
No sé la dirección de la casa
o del hotel desde donde salí.
No puedo recordarla porque simplemente no la sé.

Estoy sola y no me oriento.
Me debato tratando de rescatar edificios o
marcas en los que no me fijé.
No sé cómo volver. La angustia me despierta.

Como en los sueños no se aprende,
la pesadilla se ha repetido
a través de los años en infinitas variaciones,
y nunca puedo volver.

¿Es ésta la pesadilla de los emigrados,
de los desplazados,
de los refugiados,
de los que no pueden retornar?

MATILDE SALGANICOFF

NIGHTMARE

Again, the same dream.
I am in the street, in an unfamiliar city.
I don't know the address of the house
or the hotel I left behind.
I can't remember it because I just don't know it.

I am alone and disoriented.
I struggle trying to recognize buildings or
landmarks that I hadn't noticed before.
I don't know how to return. The anguish stirs me.

Because we don't learn in dreams,
through the years the nightmare
is repeated in infinite variations,
and I can never return.

Is this the nightmare of emigrants,
of displaced persons,
of refugees,
and of those who cannot return?

Translated by Celeste Kostopulos-Cooperman

Iluminaciones/Illuminations

TOU-VABOU

A Elihau Toker, A Héctor Yánover

Jehová evoca los signos prometidos
para evitar a los vivos
su espanto cotidiano
Únicos espectadores
anónimos y perversos
de un pueblo
que arrastra
el milagro y la duda

TOVU-VAVOHU

To Elihau Toker, to Héctor Yánover

Jehovah evokes the promised signs
to avoid the quotidian fright
of the living
The only witnesses
anonymous and perverse
of a people
who carry with them
miracles and doubt

Translated by Roberta Gordenstein

FOGO Y CINZAS

Amarrotei as cartas uma a uma
e dos sonhos desfeitos fiz o fogo
que Lilith me ensinou no paraíso
chama roubada

Mas o musgo reveste por inteiro
o irregular das pedras do meu muro,
em flor o resedá e o laranjal,

com seu perfume.

É setembro dos ventos e do pólen,
das derradeiras cinzas da lareira,
sopradas vida e morte nos caminhos
inominados.

FIRE AND EMBERS

One by one, I crushed the letters
      and of the end of my dreams I lit the fire
      taught to me by Lilith in paradise
stolen flame.

      But moss covers all
      the stones' unevenness on my wall,
      the *resedá* and the orange tree are blossoming,

      with their perfume.

      It is March of winds and pollen,
of the last embers in the fireplace,
      life and death wafted along roads
      unnamed.

Translated by Regina Igel

SEPHIROT

Numa esfera perdida un paraíso
está à minha espera não sei quando
e eu vou galgando em círculos os ramos
secos de pomos.

Os meus cabelos brancos se emaranham
disfarce dos espinhos ressequidos,
onde eu busquei romãs, maçãs e figos
do paraíso.

Perdida estou, jamais, porém, meu sonho
e a rasgada pele em gretas geme
as derradeiras gotas que alimentam
o que está morto.

SEPHIROT

In a lost sphere a paradise
waits for me I don't know when
and I go on climbing in circles the branches
dry of fruits.

My grey hair is disheveled
a mask for the dried out thorns,
where I searched for pomegranates, apples and figs
from paradise.

I'm lost, but never my dream
and my torn cracked skin moans
for the last drops that feed
what is dead.

Translated by Regina Igel

MANUSCRITO

suelen llevarlo entre oro fino molido
azul de altas torres y grana embebida
en impecable bolsa de cuero repujado
a galope de algún impaciente alazán

tocan la aldaba de manera conocida
el ritmo de los nudillos es la clave
un ligero silbido los anuncia

Solitarios
son los solitarios portadores
de la palabra nunca antes pronunciada

la que ha sido grabada en apretadas páginas
la que aún se apega a la letra
                         de derecha a izquierda

manuscrito de tensa escritura alada
entre los dedos fragmentadas las frases

límpida imagen de arroyo que corre
múltiple espejo de fuente serena

el manuscrito viaja de mano en mano:
por unos leído, por otros escuchado
por todos en la memoria preciada

de tenue polvo de estrella es la distancia
de imantadas sendas del alba es el camino

dicen que no hay recodo que no lo nombre
ni de un extremo a otro verso que lo olvide:
estepa, sabana, desierto, laguna:
entre alcázares y cúpulas de cebolla
el manuscrito no corre sino vuela:

ellos, los solitarios
                se encargan de que llegue
aún antes de la oración primera,
                aún antes del rezo del alba.

ANGELINA MUÑIZ HUBERMAN

MANUSCRIPT

they're used to carrying it in fine milled gold
blue like tall towers and engrossed garnet
in a beautiful pouch of engraved leather
on an impatient sorrel galloping fast

they sound the knocker in the accustomed manner
the rhythm of knuckles being the well known clue
a slight whistle announces their presence

lonesome
the solitary bearers
of the word never before pronounced

the word that was engraved in tight pages
the one that still goes by the letter
                         written from right to left

manuscript of tense winged writing
the sentences fragmented in between fingers

clean image of a running brook
multiple mirror of serene fountain

the manuscript goes from hand to hand:
read by some, listened to by others
and by all revered in memory

the distance is measured in slight stardust
the road goes through magnetic morning paths

they say no turning fails to name it
and no verse could forget it, from end to end:
steppe, savannah, desert, lagoon:
among palaces and onion domes
the manuscript does not run, it flies:

they, the solitary ones
                         make sure it gets there
even before the first prayer
                         even before the morning psalm.

Translated by Aurora Camacho

OBSESIÓN

Sin obsesiones
no se puede vivir,
no se puede viajar,
no se puede tomar el té,
no se puede salir al destierro.

Es la Gran Carga.
Es la Gran Riqueza.

Es la mente vuelta del revés y del derecho.

Es lo que mantiene
en pie al hombre.

En el exilio hay que ser obsesivo.

Para sobrevivir hay que ser obsesivo.

Para sobrevivir en un campo de concentración
hay que ser todavía más obsesivo.

Para ser judío hay que ser obsesivo.

Obsesivo por la vida.
Para que aún en la muerte triunfe la vida.

¿Y yo? Que tanto temo a la muerte.
Yo, sefardí de 1492 y de 1939.

Doblemente exiliada.
Doblemente judía.
Doblemente española.
Una sola vez mexicana.
Mexicana en 1942:
trasposición de 1492.

OBSESSION

Without obsessions
one cannot live
one cannot travel
one cannot have tea
one cannot go into exile.

They are the Great Burden.
They are the Great Wealth.

They are a mind turned inside out and outside in.

They are that which keeps humans
upright.

In exile one must be obsessive.

To survive one must be obsessive.

To survive in a concentration camp
one has to be even more obsessive.

To be a Jew one must be obsessive.

To be obsessive about life
so that even in death life will succeed.

And I? The one who is so afraid of death?
I, a Sephardi from 1492 and from 1939.

Twice exiled.
Twice a Jew.
Twice a Spaniard.
Only once a Mexican.
Mexican in 1942,
transposition of 1492.

Luego del exilio de Dios
y luego del exilio de la Tierra Sagrada.
Luego del exilio de pueblo en pueblo,
de ciudad en ciudad.

(De Zaragoza a Guadalajara, al Casar de Salamanca,
a Madrid, a Valencia, a Hyères, a París, a La Pallice,
al océano Atlántico, a La Habana, a Caimito
del Guayabal, a Mérida, a la ciudad de México.)
Vendrá el Gran Exilio Final.

After exile from God
after exile from the Sacred Land.
After the exile from town to town,
from city to city.

(From Zaragoza to Guadalajara, to Casar de Salamanca,
to Madrid, to Valencia, to Hyères, to Paris, to La Pallice,
to the Atlantic Ocean, to Havana, to Caimito
del Guayabal, to Merida, to Mexico City.)
The Great Final Exile will come.

Translated by Aurora Camacho

RITUAL

Enciendo mis velas.
Atrapo el secreto azul asido con ternura
al cabello blanco.

Enciendo mis velas sin observar
las sombras.
Los muros reverberan
siglos parpadeantes, ojerosos,
nauseabundos de sangre y de retórica.
Gotas. Gotas, se deslizan pálidas
por el candelabro de bronce.

Enciendo mi esperanza en la luz
y la bendigo con mis manos.
Un dorado resplandor anuncia
la caída de astros,
un principio, un final de acto.
El humo tornasol perfila una espiral.

Interminable, Dios abre sus ojos
y los cierra. Deslumbrado o aburrido
por el rito.

Enciendo mi fe con alegría,
en la creencia que ilumina mi piel
y la transforma.
Después, una feroz penumbra
rasga a dentelladas el telón.
A la insulsa realidad despierto:
astuta indiferencia del uno por el otro.

Mientras el rito de la luz se cumpla,
sigue viva la vida.
Aunque sea por entregas semanales,
persevero con mi costumbre de los viernes.

RITUAL

I light my candles.
I catch the blue secret held fast but tenderly
to the white flower stalk.

I light my candles without observing
the shadows.
The walls echo with
blinking, hollow-eyed centuries
loathsome from blood and rhetoric.
Drops. Drops gliding palely
over the bronze candelabrum.

I kindle my hope in the light
and bless it with my hands.
A golden radiance announces
the fall of heavenly bodies,
a beginning and ending of an act.
Iridescent smoke puts the finishing touches on a spiral.

Interminable, God opens his eyes
and shuts them. Dazzled or bored
by the ritual.

I light my faith with joy,
in the belief that illuminates my skin
and transforms it.
Afterwards, a ferocious half-light
slashes the curtain with its teeth.
I awaken to insipid reality:
astute indifference of one towards the other.

As long as the ritual of light is fulfilled,
life continues alive.
Even though it may be in weekly installments,
I persevere with my Friday tradition.

Translated by Roberta Gordenstein

LOS CABALISTAS

Recibieron de lo alto la voz divina,
la chispa que incendia el corazón.

La palabra sólo la tradujeron de boca a oído
Nada quedó escrito
Sobre el agua o sobre el río.

Con los nueve atributos del innombrable
más la esfera sin fin
dibujaron el árbol de la sabiduría.

La escala de la luz
El entorno en exégesis
Fuego negro en fuego blanco:
la página no dice lo que dice
sino lo que hay más allá de lo que dice.

Detenidos frente al lago,
las altas espigas en la orilla,
lanzan una piedra al punto equidistante
y los círculos concéntricos
van expurgando las vías del conocimiento.

Cada uno acoge la enseñanza que cuidadosamente bruñe
entre diamantes tallados
para el iniciado que quiera adiestrar
su sonido y su memoria

y el sueño de todas las cosas.

Angelina Muñiz Huberman

THE CABALISTS

They received from on high the divine voice
the spark that ignites the heart.

They translated the word from mouth to ear
Nothing was ever written
On the water or the river.

With the nine attributes of the unnameable
and the endless sphere
they drew the tree of wisdom.

The ladder of light
The surroundings in exegesis
Black fire on white fire:
the page does not say what it says
but what is beyond what it says.

Stopped before the lake
with high sprigs on the edge
they throw a stone to an equidistant point
and the concentric circles
begin to purify the paths to knowledge.

Each one receives the teaching that he carefully polishes
amidst finely cut diamonds
for the initiated that may want to sharpen
his sound and his memory

and the dream of all things.

Translated by Aurora Camacho

SANTUARIO

como pepitas de oro encerradas en cristal
antiguo relicario sin principio ni fin

he aquí que las vías se elevan al centro
escala de Jacob arrojada al desaire

cada uno encontraría su estela
cada uno labraría su bordón

del ancho gran morral del cielo instituido
caerían los trozos de nube devanada

seguir el camino era sólo cuestión de forma
decir adiós y nunca más volver la cabeza

ni las llagas en los pies ni las cicatrices del alma
podrían detener el lento paso de los viandantes

agua fresca que brota del manantial
milenaria sombra sobre rugoso tronco

en lo alto del monte reside el silencio del aire,
aire callado entre siete columnas elevado

al fondo el altar, desnudo altar de brazos siete:
el aire se cuela y agita labios de rezos impensados

impronunciable palabra sin eco en el santuario.

ANGELINA MUÑIZ HUBERMAN

SANCTUARY

as gold nuggets contained in crystal
ancient tabernacle without beginning or end

behold the paths rise toward the center
Jacob's ladder hurled carelessly

each one would find his trail
each one would engrave his staff

from the wide sack of an invented sky
chunks of wound-up cloud would fall

to follow the road was only a matter of form
to say good-bye and never to turn one's head

neither wounds on the feet nor scars on the soul
could possibly stop the slow step of the travelers

fresh water that surges from the spring
ancient shadow over a rugged trunk

high in the mountain the silence of air lives
stilled air by seven columns raised

and beyond the nude altar of seven arms:
air filters through and quickens lips of unthinkable prayers

unpronounceable word without echo in the sanctuary

Translated by Aurora Camacho

ABLUCIÓN

claro espejismo tras de la duna impoluta
estrellada alba del rezar estremecido
la túnica blanca se orea con los cánticos:
es un círculo no emprendido el de la tormenta

son pocos los restos del castillo en la peña
y menos los atajos que trepan hacia el monte
puñados de arena entre los ojos derramados
lento horizonte se esconde sin esperanza

las manos en la jofaina agitan el agua,
pétalos de rosa y azahar desmenuzados
suave sonido de la uña en la porcelana
ritmo de la gota de sangre entre paredes

leve tintineo de cascabeles de oro
trote de caballo a lo lejos y en la bruma

caer de la tarde y el rezo retomado

sol que se hunde y avellana triturada

límpida agua purifica la frente y los ojos
escogido elemento, sin mácula, sin huella
reúne en sí invisible sustancia de la vida
necesaria trasparencia de aire sometido

rondan los lentos perfiles en el desierto
agitan las palmas desprendidos los dátiles
no hay huella que seguir ni sendero trazado
la memoria se diluye entre granos al vuelo

al cauto devoto apresta las filacterias
sin más rumbo en la noche oscura del alma
que las parpadeantes estrellas de su rezo.

ANGELINA MUÑIZ HUBERMAN

ABLUTION

clear mirage beyond the immaculate dune
starry dawn of a trembling prayer
the white tunic is aired before the canticles:
the storm is a circle never traveled before

few are the remains of the palace on the rock
and fewer still the paths that creep toward the mountain
fistfuls of sand spilled between the eyes
slow horizon that hides without hope

the hands in the basin make the water shudder,
minced petals of rose and orange blossom
soft sound of a fingernail against the porcelain
rhythm of a drop of blood between the walls

light jingling of golden bells
a horse trotting far away in the mist

the fall of evening and prayer resumed

a sun that sinks and ground hazelnut

limpid water purifies forehead and eyes
chosen element, spotless, without a trace
gathers in itself the blind substance of life
the necessary clarity of subjugated air

the slow silhouettes hover in the desert
loosened clusters of dates make palm trees quake
there are no footprints to follow, no marked path
memory is diluted amid flying seeds

the wary devotee readies his phylacteries
with no other destination in the dark night of the soul
but the blinking stars of his own supplication.

Translated by Aurora Camacho

LOS RABINOS CABALISTAS

Entonces, inventaron alfabetos.
Del uno nació el alef,
soberano indivisible.
El dos nació del uno:
bet, *dualidad de sexos*
más el uno, gimmel, *tres.*
Del tríangulo primario
saltó Adán,
del polvo al arquetipo.

Después, crearon al Golem.
A Dios imitar quisieron
en permutación de letras.
Le grabaron rotundo mensaje:
la grave santidad del monigote
aplastó al rabino con enfado.
Locura y éxtasis mezclaron en burbujas.

ROSITA KALINA

THE CABALISTIC RABBIS

Next they invented alphabets.
From one the *aleph* was born,
indivisible sovereign.
Two was born from one:
bet, duality of sexes
plus one, *gimmel*, three.
From the primary triangle
leapt Adam,
from dust to the archetype.

Later, they created the Golem.
They tried to imitate God
in the permutation of letters.
They engraved an unequivocal message for Him:
The weighty sanctity of the lay-brother
angrily crushed the rabbi.
Madness and ecstasy blended together into bubbles.

Translated by Roberta Gordenstein

TODA ILUSIÓN ES UNA FORMA DE ESPERANZA

y la fe no sabe de razones.
En algún trazo escondido de la Escritura
se encuentra el destino humano, la esfera luminosa, la matriz,
la herida del error y la semilla temprana de la
redención.
Dios con el hombre, el hombre con su dios
como una mitad con su mitad de luz
intentando, tanteando, apenas tocando
ser
en existencia real;
sentir
con goce minucioso
la porfiada luz célica
que se vuelve grito erecto
que busca la salida de su cuerpo;
hacer
en un presente único
en libre acto de amor,
            —en su error, su miedo y maravilla—
con los íntimos frutos perplejos
en trabajo desasido de la nada
como un papel abierto
que espera ser cavado desde adentro
en forma nueva
colmando el vuelo a tropezones.

AIDA GELBTRUNK

ALL ILLUSION IS A FORM OF HOPE

and faith knows nothing of reasons.
In some hidden tracing of Scripture
you can find human destiny, the luminous sphere, the womb,
the wound of error and the early seed of
redemption.
God with man, man with his god
like one half with its half of light
attempting, testing, barely touching,
to be
in actual existence;
to feel
with minute pleasure
the stubborn celestial light
that becomes an erect cry
that seeks the exit from its body;
to create
in a unique present
in a free act of love,
            —in its error, its fear and marvel—
with the intimate perplexed fruits
in work released from nothingness
like a blank sheet of paper
that waits to be dug out from within
in a new form
filling the flight by fits and starts.

Translated by Roberta Gordenstein

EL CÍRCULO DEL GOLEM

*El rabino Eleazar abrió la palma de la mano
y dejó escapar la tierra virgen prodigiosa
Tomó agua pura de la fuente de la montaña
Recitó las doscientas veintiuna combinaciones alfabéticas
y formó el golem.*

*Quiso que el hombre de barro caminara
y el hombre de barro caminó
Quiso que el hombre de barro obedeciera
y el hombre de barro obedeció
Quiso que trabajara, limpiara y ordenara
y trabajó, limpió y ordenó.*

*Quiso hablar con él y quiso que tuviera un alma:
silencio:
el gólem desmoronó su polvo y al polvo regresó.*

*El rabino Eleazar recordó
que todos los hombres son mortales.*

ANGELINA MUÑIZ HUBERMAN

THE CIRCLE OF THE GOLEM

Rabbi Eleazar opened the palm of his hand
and let go of the virginal prodigious soil
He took pure water from the mountain spring
He recited the two hundred and twenty-one combinations of letters
and he formed the golem.

He meant the man of clay to walk
and the man of clay walked
He meant the man of clay to obey
and the man of clay obeyed
He meant him to work, to clean up, to create order
and he worked, and cleaned up, and created order.

He meant to talk to him and to give him a soul:
silence:
the golem crumbled and returned to the dust.

Then Rabbi Eleazar remembered
that all men are mortals.

Translated by Aurora Camacho

ANGELINA MUÑIZ HUBERMAN

EL OJO DE LA CREACIÓN

Igual que corre el ibis blanco
sobre la hierba que no pisa
y tres gotas de sangre granan su plumaje
de suave curva

—tres gotas de sangre que no se ven—
y el olor salobre del agua pescadera
se confunde en el olor del semen milenario

Igual que corre la sombra al encuentro
del cuerpo olvidado
y se dobla en lo oculto del terreno quebradizo

Igual que el aire se afana entre los canales
perdidos de las dunas arrastradas

Igual que suena la hora última
—aunque el muerto no la oiga—
y suena la gota destilada del amor
—aunque subterránea no aflore—

Corre, se dobla, se afana y suena
el escondido río de las aguas plácidas
del ojo de la creación.

Angelina Muñiz Huberman

THE EYE OF CREATION

Just as the white ibis runs
on grass it does not stand on
and three drops of blood enliven its plumage
                              in soft curve

—three invisible drops of blood—
and the salty smell of fish water
is confused with the odor of ancient semen

As the shadow runs to meet
          the forgotten body
and it folds in the hidden parts of the fragile ground

As the air strives between the lost canals
of dragged dunes

As the last hour sounds
—although the dead man cannot hear it—
and the distilled drop of love sounds
—even though it doesn't blossom underground—

The hidden river of tranquil waters
runs, breaks, strives, sounds
              from the eye of creation.

Translated by Aurora Camacho

GOLEM Y RABINO III

¿Quién somete? ¿Y quién es sometido? Dícese que en cierta ocasión (esta historia sucedió, con variantes, muchas veces) el que se rebeló no fue el Golem sino su Amo. Te prohíbo que me obedezcas, gritó con voz terrible. Y el Golem se vio forzado a realizar la más difícil de las tareas: ser amo de sí mismo. En cambio su Creador, liberado al fin, se dedicó entonces a obedecer puntualmente las órdenes de su suegra.

ANA MARÍA SHÚA

GOLEM AND RABBI III

Who subdues? And who is subdued? This story is told, with variations, many times; however, legend has it that one time the one who rebelled was not the Golem but his Master. I forbid you to obey me, he shouted in a horrible voice. And the Golem was forced to accomplish the most difficult task of all: to be his own master. On the other hand his Creator, free at last, devoted himself to obeying his mother-in-law's every wish and command.

Translated by Rhonda Buchanan

GOLEM Y RABINO IV

*¡No me obedezcas!—ordenó su Amo al perplejo Golem que,
ansioso por cumplir su orden, la desobedeció al instante,
mostrándose aun más servil que de costumbre.*

ANA MARÍA SHÚA

GOLEM AND RABBI IV

Don't obey me!—the Master ordered the perplexed Golem who, anxious to fulfill his command, disobeyed it immediately, showing himself to be even more subservient than ever.

Translated by Rhonda Buchanan

GOLEM Y RABINO V

Se toma un trozo de arcilla, se la moldea dándole la forma de un ser humano, se realizan ciertos ritos, se pronuncian ciertas fórmulas, se sopla en la boca de la estatua el aliento vital y la estatua no se mueve ni le crecen las uñas o el cabello, se verifica en el Libro el pasaje correspondiente en busca de algún error, pero cuando se intenta repetir el ritual, el Hombre de Barro ha desaparecido. Se toma otro trozo de arcilla, se la moldea, veintisiete Golems fugitivos, veintisiete errores acechan en las sombras, repiten a coro los salmos para confundir al rabino, qué difícil inscribir así en la arcilla blanda, oh señor, oh señor ayúdame, la fórmula cromosómica completa.

GOLEM AND RABBI V

You take a piece of clay and mold it, shaping it into a human being; certain rituals are performed, certain phrases pronounced. The breath of life is blown into the mouth of the statue, but the statue doesn't move nor do its fingernails or hair grow. You check the appropriate passage in the Book looking for an error, but when you try to repeat the ritual, the Man of Clay has disappeared. So you take another piece of clay and mold it: twenty-seven fugitive Golems, twenty-seven errors lurk in the shadows repeating the psalms in unison to confuse the rabbi. It's so hard, oh God, oh God help me, to inscribe the complete chromosomal formula in soft clay.

Translated by Rhonda Buchanan

ES TEMPRANO AÚN

Es temprano aún,
me dicen,
y vuelvo la mirada hacia atrás
y veo pedazos de vida
aquí y allá, dispersos, exhaustos.

Tienes el blanco y el negro en tus manos,
me dicen,
y miro hacia adelante
y una impávida oscuridad
cubre la luz temblorosa.

Las palabras nacen y caen en el papel
sembrando frases ilusorias.
Apenas suenan en los oídos:
perdieron su ritmo interno.

La música murió en el tumulto.
El aroma de la flor se extravió
en el laberinto de las especias.
Mas es temprano aún,
me dicen,
y crece la incertidumbre
ante las horas que llegan.

ELVIRA LEVY

IT IS STILL EARLY

It is still early,
they tell me,
and I turn my glance backwards
and see pieces of life
here and there, scattered, exhausted.

You have black and white in your hands,
they tell me,
and I look forward,
and an unflinching darkness
covers the tremulous light.

Words are born and fall on the paper
sowing illusory phrases.
They barely sound in your ears:
they have lost their internal rhythm.

The music died in the tumult.
The flower's aroma got lost
in the labyrinth of spices.
But it is still early,
they tell me,
and uncertainty grows
before the approaching hours.

Translated by Roberta Gordenstein

La textura de la memoria/
The Texture of Memory

DESIERTO I

Como una ráfaga que hechiza el verbo
se abre tu lirio cada tarde
y anuncia el sagrado ritual de los caminantes

y es: El comienzo de los comienzos

Crepúsculo del génesis en la visión del poeta
Un hálito de piedra
que recuerda el primer día

MONICA MANSUR

DESERT I

Like a flash of light that bewitches the word
your lily blossoms every afternoon
and announces the sacred ritual of the travelers

and it is: The beginning of beginnings

Twilight of genesis in the poet's vision
a breath of stone
that recalls the first day

Translated by Celeste Kostopulos-Cooperman

MI MEMORIA

mi memoria se desnuda por las noches
los vestidos caen suavemente
rodeando sus pies
la ropa interior se queda pegada
casi una con el cuerpo
y hay que arrancar broches y sedas
encajes y ataduras
hasta que sólo brille la piel

y así   de pie
palpa su fuerza contra el mundo
el resplandor del secreto en carne viva
las palabras sin desollar

una persiana la divide en franjas de luz
en su vientre se gesta el sol

MÓNICA MANSUR

MY MEMORY

my memory disrobes at night
the clothes fall softly
encircling her feet
the underwear remains attached
almost one with her body
and one must tear off clasps and silks
laces and fastenings
until only the skin is shining

and so   standing
she tests her strength against the world
the splendor of the secret in living flesh
words without flaying

a venetian blind divides her into bands of light
in her womb the sun gestates

Translated by Maria Xirinachs

FALSO DISCURSO

"É tão bom estar só,
          vagar a esmo pela minha casa
que fala das lembranças
          sem possíveis partilhas…"
Em solilóquio eu mesma me convenço.

"Como é bom estar só!
          Pinçar aquela foto esmaecida
do baralho escondido,
captura do que fomos."
Em solilóquio eu mesma me convenço.

          "Mais que nunca estar só!
          Ir ao jardim, colher fruto maduro
no almoço improvisado
à mesa, sem convivas."
Em solilóquio eu mesma me convenço.

"Para sempre, estar só.
          Rolar na cama grande desgranhada,
          e como um animal
sem máscara dormindo."
Em solilóquio eu mesma me convenço.

Eternamente só.
          Nos parques onde os pares se entrelaçam,
a falsa persuasão
inútil se recolhe
          e o solilóquio aos prantos se soterra.

LEONOR SCLIAR-CABRAL

DECEIVING WORDS

"It feels so good to be by myself,
        to wander through my house
that speaks of memories
        exempt of divisions…"
In a soliloquy I convince myself of that.

"How good it is to be by myself!
        To fetch that faded out picture
in a hidden deck of cards,
a glimpse of what we were."
In a soliloquy I convince myself of that.

        "More than ever, to be by myself!
        To go to the orchard, to grab a ripe fruit
in the improvised lunch
at a table, without guests."
In a soliloquy I convince myself of that.

"For ever, to be by myself.
        To roll over on the big bed disheveled,
        and like an animal
sleeping with no mask."
In a soliloquy I convince myself of that.

By myself for eternity.
        In parks where couples embrace,
the false persuasion
useless curls itself in
        and the soliloquy is flooded by tears.

Translated by Regina Igel

LAS TRENZAS DE LA TORAH

El pelito para Yom Kippur *atado de fiesta*
a un vestido de terciopelo azul trenzas
seda dulce de las trenzas hebreas o
es en el baño de la sinagoga
donde las señoras
descompuestas se lavan la cara el sombrero
descompuesto también de afeites
en el espejo espiando como madrinas
no como madres se acomodan
a la religión de sus familias
mujeronas de cartera pesada
a mí me empujan.
La nena del pelito judía
Tamara o Tamar
cómo la llaman
cuando hay que volver
sí tía espérame
ya voy ya me hago de miedo
la que rezo.

TORAH BRAIDS

Her beautiful hair for Yom Kippur festively tied
to a dress of blue velvet braids
sweet silk of Hebrew braids or
it is in the bathroom of the synagogue
where ladies
in disarray cleanse their faces of make-up
their hats in disarray also
in the mirror spying like godmothers
not like mothers they adapt
to the religion of their families
matrons with heavy purses
pushing me.
The young girl with beautiful Jewish hair
Tamara or Tamar
as they call her
when we must return
yes aunt wait for me
I'm coming I'm peeing in fear
the one who prays.

Translated by Roberta Gordonstein

ELIAHU

Cuando dijiste el Shmá Israel que cada vez quiso decir
otra cosa esperamos muchos minutos y él no llegaba, él que
no era nada (o bien era etéreo) pero hacía ruido
y se tomaba la copa de vino del medio de la mesa, él que te secaba
las manos que año por medio me tocaba lavarte, la palangana
preparada, terror a volcar el agua, risas contenidas
cuando las bendiciones eran cada vez más agudas, y yo
mirando la copa que no se vaciaba. Y sin embargo parecía
vaciarse hasta imaginar que él se emborracharía un poco
en cada casa, tomando de cada copa alta, única, brillante
en el centro de cada mesa. Millones de copas únicas esperando
en millones de mesas festivas y él que entró sin ser
visto cuando se abrieron las puertas que se le cerraron detrás.
Yo que estuve controlando sus pasos. Nuevamente
este año escuchamos el cuento del pan que siempre es otro
cuento, y de nuevo preguntamos las cuatro preguntas espiando
las pequeñas letras hebreas de olor a baúl, de olor
a viaje desde Rusia, a las barbas del bisabuelo Akiva que
espió la ceremonia desde el marco ovalado con su sombrero redondo.
Nadie supo nunca si las últimas canciones de la noche
eran las que él había inventado cuando se sentaba inclinándose
a recibir el shabat en la silla alta que guardaste hasta
que hijo por hijo se fueron yendo de la casa con corredor,
con terraza, con biblioteca de puertas de vidrio, con anchas
biblias olorosas, con los vestidos del casamiento en Brasil
cuando bajaron con náuseas del barco que después siguió
y llegó a Buenos Aires. Dos noches seguidas se repite la
ceremonia, en Europa se repite tres noches, algunas sectas
la hacen una sola vez pero cantan más alto, también
bailan. Nosotros a veces levantamos los brazos hacia el
cielo cantando alto y eso es tan importante como decir el
Shmá Israel siete veces antes de dormir, para adentro, nunca
en voz alta. Vergüenza de la propia voz diciendo Shmá
Israel. Sabiendo desde siempre que aunque sólo se pensara
sería escuchando, porque él escucha todos los hermosos pensamientos
y contesta en los pensamientos mismos como nadie puede hacerlo.

TAMARA KAMENSZAIN

ELIAHU

When you said the Shema Yisroel that meant something different each time we waited a long while and he did not arrive, the one who was nothing (or rather was ethereal), but made noise and drank the glass of wine from the middle of the table, he who dried your hands that every other year it was my duty to wash, the wash-basin prepared, fear of spilling the water, laughter contained when each time the blessings became sharper, and I kept watching the cup that did not empty. And nevertheless it seemed to empty itself until I imagined that he would get a little drunk in each house, drinking from each tall glass, unique, brilliant in the center of each table. Millions of different glasses waiting on millions of festive tables and the one who entered without being seen when they opened the doors that were closed behind him. I was the one controlling his steps. Again this year we heard the story of the matzo that is always another story, and again we asked the four questions scrutinizing the small Hebrew letters that smelled like a trunk, like a journey from Russia, like the whiskers of great-grandfather Akiva wearing his round hat who contemplated the ceremony from the oval picture frame.

No one ever knew if the final songs of the night were the ones he invented when he sat down, reclining, to welcome the Sabbath in the tall chair that you saved until one by one the children began going from the house with a hallway, with a terrace, with a library with glass doors, with thick and odorous Bibles, with the garments from the wedding in Brazil when they disembarked seasick from the ship that afterwards continued on until it reached Buenos Aires. The ceremony is repeated on two consecutive nights, in Europe it is repeated three nights, some sects do it a single time but they sing louder, they dance, too. We sometimes raise our arms up to heaven singing loudly and that is as important as saying the Shema Yisroel seven times before sleeping, to yourself, never out loud. Ashamed by hearing your own voice saying Shema Yisroel. Always knowing that even if you only thought it, it would be heard, because he hears all the beautiful thoughts and answers in the same thoughts the way no one else can.

Nadie más que Adonai o Eliahu Hanaví que tomó de la copa alta, te secó las manos que este año me tocó lavarte, y sin hacer ruido cruzó por la ventana abierta y entró por la puerta abierta de cualquier casa donde la copa de vino lo esperaba en el centro de la mesa.

No one other than Adonai or Eliahu Hanavi who drank from the tall glass, dried your hands that this year it was my turn to wash, and without making noise passed through the open window and entered the open door of any house where the glass of wine awaited him in the center of the table.

Translated by Roberta Gordenstein

RETORNO II

Desde que se pegó el otoño a las calles húmedas de esta
ciudad reconocible a través de los tangos no puedo más
que caminar con los brazos pegados al pecho tratando de
ubicarme en el día exacto de mi nacimiento porque desde
hoy sé que los que bendijeron mi nombre con un rezo tomaban
vino dulce en copitas y comían pescado frito para
acostumbrar su alma a la presencia de una nueva alma
que entonces no era más que un punto entre árboles, un
soplo entre sólidos alientos, un gesto entre risas
perfectamente nítidas.

    Desde que se pegó el otoño a las calles húmedas de esta
ciudad reconocible a través de los tangos, vuelvo a preguntarme
por las primeras alegrías por las imágenes que
llenaron una pupila aún no acostumbrada a la luz por los
primeros contactos de la lengua con la solidez del mundo.
Vuelvo a preguntarme por el sentido de todo lo que mágicamente
existe hace veinticinco años desenvolviéndose
con la naturalidad con que se pela una naranja y entiendo
que cuando más se quiera saber menos se sabrá porque
están cerrados los caminos que descienden del árbol a la raíz.

    En esta tristeza de no ser más la que sentándose en las
rodillas de un abuelo escuchaba la historia de la moabita
Ruth está la alegría de encontrar en cada objeto un indicio
de esta historia, el asombro de saber que la poesía
no hace más que continuarla porque es a la vez la madre
y la hija de la moabita Ruth.

    Es la gran madre en cuyo vientre se genera el complicado
tejido de palabras, es la hija que surge de ese vientre
para reposar en la intemperie de la imaginación, en el
esclavizado y libre campo del recuerdo.

RETURN II

Since autumn attached itself to the humid streets of this city
recognizable because of the tangos I can only stroll with my arms
stuck to my chest, trying to place myself on the exact day of my
birth because from now on I know that those who blessed my name
with a prayer drank sweet wine in shot glasses and ate fried fish
to accustom their souls to the presence of a new soul that was
then no more than a speck among trees, a puff among strong breath-
ing, a gesture among perfectly neat laughter.

Since autumn attached itself to the humid streets of this city
recognizable because of the tangos, I ask myself again about the
earliest joys about the images that filled a pupil still not
accustomed to the light about the first contact of the tongue
with the solidness of the world. I ask myself again about the
meaning of all that magically existed twenty-five years ago
developing itself with the naturalness with which one peels an
orange and I understand that the more you want to know the less
you will know because the paths that descend from the tree to the
root are closed.

In this sadness of no longer being the one who sits on her
grandfather's knees listening to the story of Ruth the Moabite is
the joy of finding a trace of that story in every object, the
astonishment of knowing that poetry only continues it because it is
at one and the same time the mother and daughter of Ruth the
Moabite.

She is the great mother in whose womb the complicated
weaving of words is generated, she is the daughter who emerges
from that womb to rest in the openness of the imagination, in the
enslaved and free field of memory.

Mi abuelo decía que mientras Ruth peregrinaba por los
caminos de la tierra santa sus ojos—fijos en el cielo—
vaticinaban las lluvias, dialogaban con los vientos y abrían
el espacio necesario para que aparezcan las nubes.

Toda historia abre un espacio en el que podemos acomodar
nuestros cuerpos haciendo la plancha sobre un mundo
de personajes cuyas correrías dependen del destino
azaroso de las palabras. Sin la historia del abuelo no hay
Ruth pero sin Ruth no hay lluvias ni diálogo con los vientos
ni polvorientos caminos de Moab por los que se bambolean
camellos cargados de telas, de especias orientales,
de pálidos niños que serán vendidos como esclavos y verán
su vida como una monótona estela arrastrándose detrás
de los remos que deben empujar.

My grandfather used to say that while Ruth wandered through the paths of the Holy Land her eyes—fixed on heaven— prophesied the rains, dialogued with the winds, and opened the necessary space so the clouds would appear.

Every story opens a space where we can accommodate our bodies and lose ourselves in a world of characters whose wanderings depend on the hazardous destiny of words. Without grandfather's story there is no Ruth but without Ruth there is no rain or dialogue with the winds or dusty roads of Moab where camels sway loaded down with fabrics, with oriental spices, with pale children who will be sold as slaves and who will see their lives as a monotonous wake dragged behind the oars that they must push.

Translated by Roberta Gordenstein

MEA SHEARIM

Besé a la tierra fría que es cielo y supe que la flor era sagrada
como el sol, como las escaleras del barrio de las cien
puertas invisibles, que conducen a la eternidad sin nombre.
    Entendí por qué sus habitantes se llaman "los cuidadores
de la ciudad," supe que cuidaban una ciudad invisible para mí.

    Y ahora quisiera alabar el polvo de los zapatos hundidos
en escritos antiguos, quedarme con el espejo de lo que está
vivo reflejándose en mil espejos, la imagen absurda de lo que
me rodea cuando me despierto (cuando mi imagen se despierta)
(que es como decir aleluya) que es como abrir una caja redonda
y reencontrar el celeste el amarillo el celeste, que es tratar de
abrir una caja redonda y encontrarse con el cuadrado que rodea
o invade y no deja ver el infinito inmenso que Heráclito envió ayer
en una luz, desde Efeso en Turquía (ciudad invadida por los mares),
que siendo cada vez otros son los mismos porque están encerrados
en una caja redonda y conducen a la eternidad sin nombre (aquella
que quiere y no quiere ser llamada con el nombre de Zeus).

Me vienen a la memoria aquellas caras que un poeta llamó
"trabajadas por el tiempo." Las arrugas surcando los ojos
amarillentos de mi padre están en la pantalla de esta pared
para recordarme la muerte.
    Filas de antepasados haciendo una ronda que se tragará
a todos los hijos, una ronda inmóvil en la que los pasos de sus habitantes
no avanzan, en la que no veo los ojos que el niño
Cupido envió en una flecha para que un gesto único se vaya
repitiendo en la galería tecnicolor de mi mente.

El recuerdo de ese gesto generará la ronda de la vida
en la que mis antepasados bailen borrachos
y las arrugas del padre indiquen la sabiduría
y las manos ajadas de la abuela sean signo
de haber pasado por un ritual doméstico pero santo.

MEA SHEARIM

I kissed the cold earth that is heaven and discovered that the flower was sacred like the sun, like the invisible stairways of the *neighborhood of the hundred doors*, which lead to an eternity without name.

I understood why its inhabitants are called "the caretakers of the city," learned that they cared for a city invisible to me.

And now I would like to praise the dust of the shoes submerged in ancient writings, remain with the mirror of what is alive reflecting itself in a thousand mirrors, the absurd image of what surrounds me when I awaken (when my image awakens) (which is like saying hallelujah) that is like opening a round box and finding again the celestial the yellow the celestial, that is trying to open a round box and finding oneself with the square that surrounds or invades and does not permit seeing the immense infinity that Heraclitus sent yesterday in a light, from Efeso in Turkey (city invaded by the seas), that being every time others are still the same because they are trapped in a round box and lead to eternity without name (that one that wants and does not want to be called by the name of Zeus).

Those faces that a poet called "forged by time" come to memory. The wrinkles furrowing the yellowish eyes of my father are on the screen of this wall to remind me of death.

Lines of ancestors making the rounds that will devour all their children, an immobile patrol where the steps of its inhabitants do not advance, where I do not see the eyes that boy Cupid sent in an arrow so that a unique gesture will continue to repeat in the technicolor gallery of my mind.

The memory of that gesture will generate the serenade of life
where my drunken ancestors dance
and my father's wrinkles indicate wisdom
and my grandmother's faded hands are the sign
of having passed through a domestic but holy ritual.

Nuevamente hay un tiempo para morir y un tiempo para vivir
una mano sobre un seno despierta las corrientes dormidas del cuerpo
el arco de una rodilla siembra la alegría,
abre para las mariposas un espacio infinito en el cual circular.

Again there is a time to live and a time to die
a hand on a breast awakens the sleeping currents of the body
the arch of a knee sows happiness.
An infinite space opens for butterflies to circulate in.

Translated by Roberta Gordenstein

Desde YISKOR

57.
¿Me oyes? Debajo de mi nombre estoy yo
La pequeña olvidada dice que no sabe   dice que no sabe
Loba ¿estás allí?
Y para recordarme vuelvo a ti
Qué sola debes sentirte
(esto es sólo el testimonio del oyente)

59.
Escucho a través de paredes subterráneas como los presos se dan señales
unos a otros
Memoria ¿me oyes?
Creces como lo que se olvida
Y aquella que soy ofrece perdón a la que fui

60.
Sobre la mesa unas fotografías
Esa muchacha la de la izquierda al frente sí, esa soy yo

61.
El corazón
Crater
Testigo
Contesta
Contéstame
La voz pálida
Cae
Las palabras desfondadas
Caen
Inscripciones
Fechas
Las muertes y lo que de ellas nace
No expliques
Perdida en ti

From YISKOR

Author's note: Yiskor *derives from the Hebrew root* zahor, *which I take to mean "to remember." as in the prayer that begins "Remember, O Lord, the soul that has passed on to eternal life." The* Yiskor *is recited four times a year.*

57.
Can you hear me? under my name I am
The little lost one says she does not know   does not know
                                        She-wolf: are you there?
To remember I turn to you
What a loneliness you must feel
              (This is only the testimony of the one who listens)

59.
I listen through underground walls like prisoners signaling
To one another
                    Memory: can you hear me?
You grow, like some forgotten thing
And what I am forgives what I have been

60.
On the table a few photographs
That girl on the left in the front—it's me alright

61.
The heart
              A crater
Witness
        Answer
                        Answer me
The pale voice
              Falls
The bottomless words
                    Fall
Inscriptions
        Dates
Deaths and what they gave birth to

                    Don't explain

Whatever was lost in you

Tú

No expliques
Cada año
    Yiskor
63.

  Ella llora
    Sin tocarla en un acto reflejo lloro con ella
      Busco el lugar del corazón

Los gritos se pierden en lo oscuro del sueño en la oscuridad de la noche
en lo oscuro de la casa   en la opacidad del silencio
La mañana se sostiene por las paredes verde pálido
Somos los que se van

68.

Desembarcamos un mediodía en el puerto Veracruz. Trajimos abrigos
gruesos de piel. En La Habana comí mango por primera vez. ¿A quién
contarle esto?

Memoria del mar y su tedio, de la muchacha que fui. El vestido gris que
ahora se ve ridículo en la fotografía. Memoria de las tablas percudidas
del barco, de aquellas olas impávidas, caducas en su belleza. Memoria de
la luna casi insoportable

Es mediodía. Es hoy. Desembarco. Es un día de agosto
Jamás me había sentido tan aferrada a la vida

73.

Ella se arranca de su sombra. Es una mujer vieja y sigue siendo hermosa.
Las palabras no alcanzan. Su piel ha sido devastada por la falta de
caricias. Tampoco hay ruido. La vida es el único refugio. Estar aquí para
nadie. Para nada. Ah, cómo te moriste en mí

74.

La tierra se deshiela. No sé por qué esta mañana me quedará para
siempre. Es el olor de los lirios arrancándose a la nieve (en realidad es
una mañana igual a las demás) ¿Por qué es ésta la que guardo?

                    You
Don't explain
Each year
          Yiskor

63.

          She is crying
          In sudden impulse, I too cry with her
                    I am searching for the heart's space

The weeping is lost in the dark of the dream in the darkness of night
in the dark of the house   in the opacity of silence
The morning holds to the pale green walls
We are the ones leaving

68.

We docked at noon in the port of Veracruz. We wore our Russian
furs. In Havana I tasted a mango for the first time. Who can recount
all this?

Memories of the sea and its weariness, of the girl I was. The gray
dress that seems so preposterous now in the photo. Memory of the
stained boards of the boat, impervious to waves, perishable in its
beauty. Memory of the moon—nearly unendurable.

It is noon. It is today. I dock. It is an August day
I have never felt so anchored in my life

73.

She detaches herself from her shadow. She is an old woman and still
beautiful. Words do not reach her. Her skin has already been damaged
by the lack of caresses. Neither is there any sound. Life is the only
refuge. To be here for nobody. For nothing. Oh, how can you have
died inside me!

74.

The earth thaws. I do not know why this morning lingers forever. It
is the smell of irises sprung from the snow (actually it is a morning
like any other). Why do I brood over this one?

115

75.

Una mujer con un vestido gris. Un recuerdo apenas para unos cuantos que acabarán por olvidarla. Algunas tardes compartidas que se asemejarán a otras, los crepúsculos, la mañana de un día caluroso. Tercos sueños, dávidas para nadie apenas para ella misma. La fotografía no nos descubre nada, (todavía es una mujer joven). Yo nunca la conocí.

76.

Aquella muchacha sola en el muelle
Esta imagen para siempre
¿Qué vida fue ésta?
¿Y qué es lo que quiero decir?

Mi voz se confunde con la tuya
El verano se desborda   los pájaros se golpean contra la luz

Y yo no puedo despertar

80.

El silencio es un trabajo que durará toda su vida. Ocurre en lo más profundo, en lo más oscuro como una enfermedad mortal.

¿Yo? ¿Esta mujer soy yo?

83.

Nada   no me dices nada
Tú me escuchas
La hora del dolor ha pasado

Nada   no queda nada
Tú que me escuchas ¿todavía reconoces a la que fui?
Soy yo la que puede morir en cualquier momento

75.

The woman in a gray dress. Barely a memory, for the few who will
finally forget her. Some shared evenings that look like any other.
Dawn of a hot day. Difficult dreams, gifts for nobody, much less for
her. The photograph yields no clues (she's still a young woman). I
never knew her.

76.

This girl alone on the pier

This eternal image

What life was that?

And what might this mean?

My voice mingles with yours
The summer overflows   birds throw themselves against the light

And I cannot waken

80.

Silence is a task that will last all her life. It continues
in the depths, in the darkness, like a mortal illness

And I? Am I that woman?

83.

Nothing   you tell me nothing
                         You who are listening for me
                         The grieving time is over

Nothing   absolutely nothing remains
                 you who are listening for me, Do you still recognize
                         who I was? I who could die at any moment

el diagrama de la lluvia

El tedio de la espera
el movimiento de los sueños
el pasto cubierto de hojas secas

85.

Acaso somos la misma oscuridad las mismas palabras

los mismos gritos

Nunca lo sabrás Los muertos no entienden a los vivos

Y si hasta tus fauces
Y si fuera hasta el remordimiento
Tú que ya no me escuchas
Tú que ya no me oyes llorar
Abreme el perdóna cógeme en tu indiferencia

La tierra te ha deshecho
No sabes que estoy aquí

La lluvia arrecia Se parte como las aguas del Estigia
Nada que temer Somos cómplices

no te debo nada concédeme tu olvido

¿Dónde está tu muerte ahora?

87.

¿Y qué buscabas en aquel sueño?
Ten piedad de aquellos que ya han vivido su vida
Dame la añoranza para que pueda buscarte en lo profundo de las

cisternas

Todo cuanto he amado desapareció

Estoy cercada
Ruega por mí

                              The tedium of hope
the diagram of the rain   the motion of dreams
                              the lawn littered with dry leaves

85.

Maybe we are the same darkness   the same words
                                               the same cries
      You'll never know it   The dead don't comprehend the living

                              And if it came to your very jaws
                                    And if it came to remorse
                              You who no longer listen for me
                              You who no longer hear my cries
         Hold out some mercy for me   Shelter me in your indifference

The earth has undone you
You do not know I am here
            The rain falls harder   It opens like the waters of the Styx.
            Fear nothing   We are accomplices
               I owe you nothinggrant me your oblivion

                                       Where is your death now?

87.
                 And what were you searching for, in that dream?
Have mercy for those who lived their lives
Grant me the aching to search for you through the depth of
                                                      wells
All I have loved has vanished
                        I am walled in
                        Pray for me

                              Translated by Stephen Tapscott

TODO NO ES SINO TIEMPO

Todo no es sino tiempo
Allá donde unas cuantas buganvillas en un vaso de agua
bastan para hacernos un jardín
Porque morimos solos. Y la muerte es apenas el despertar
de este sueño primero de vivir y dijo mi abuela a la salida del cine
sueña que es hermoso el sueño de la vida, muchacha
Se oxida la lumbre de las veladoras
y yo, ¿dónde estoy?
Soy la que fui siempre. Lo inesperado de estar siendo
Llego al lugar del principio donde comienza el comienzo
Este es el tiempo
Es el tiempo del despertar
La abuela enciende las velas sabáticas desde su muerte y me mira
Se extiende el sábado hasta nunca, hasta después, hasta antes
Mi abuela que murió de sueños
mece interminablemente el sueño que la inventa
que yo invento. Una niña loca me mira desde adentro

LIFE IS NOTHING BUT TIME

Life is nothing but time:
There a few sprigs of bougainvillea in a vase of water
are enough—to make a garden.
Because we die alone. And because death is enough to awaken us
from this first dream of living, and my grandmother said
      as we left the movies
Dream,for it is lovely, muchacha, the dream of life
The candle flame rusts
and I, where am I?
I am that which always was. The surprise of being
I am back to the place of origin, where the beginning begins
This is the time
It is the time of awakening
The old woman lights her Sabbath candles from her death and she
      watches me
The Sabbath expands until never, until after, until before
My grandmother who died of dreams
endlessly stirs the dream that she invents,
that I invent. A wild girl watches me from my inmost self.

Translated by Stephen Tapscott

ALEJANDRA PIZARNIK

ESTAR

Vigilas desde este cuarto
donde la sombra temible es la tuya.

No hay silencio aquí
sino frases que evitas oír.

Signos en los muros
narran la bella lejanía.

(Haz que no muera
sin volver a verte.)

EXISTING

You keep watch from this room
where the fearful shadow is your own.

There is no silence here
but phrases you avoid hearing.

Signs on the walls
narrate the beautiful remoteness.

(Don't let me die
without seeing you again.)

Translated by Roberta Gordenstein

LINTERNA SORDA

Los ausentes soplan y la noche es densa. La noche
tiene el color de los párpados del muerto.
Toda la noche hago la noche. Toda la noche escribo.
Palabra por palabra yo escribo la noche.

ALEJANDRA PIZARNIK

DEAF LANTERN

The absent ones whisper and the night is dense. Night is the
color of the eyelids of the dead.
All night long I create the night. All night long I write.
Word by word I write the night.

Translated by Celeste Kostopulos-Cooperman

A ANA FRANK

Señor, hazme digna del número.
Recuerda, como ayer, que ardiente flecha
atraviesa la tierra.
Mi cruz se clava iracunda
en tus arcanos.

Desnuda caminó mi pena
por el infértil campo del acero y la metralla.
Toqué violín en Auschwitz,
alegre canto, Novena Sinfonía,
luces que Beethoven dirigía melancólico,
entre apagados semitonos y sordera.

Treblinka me abrió los muslos de la impiedad.
¿Acaso soñé dramas o inventé amarguras,
para congraciarme con el mundo?

Ni santa. Ni heroína.
Mi desnuda piel ha visto demasiado
de estos tiempos iracundos.
¿Es que acaso vendrá el Apocalipsis
cuando mi sagrado número
se borre ante Tus ojos?

Ciento dieciocho mil. Número de suerte
luce mi antebrazo. Sello Santo.
Vuelo, vuelo de mi gracia. Más arriba.
Arriba. Salta, salta la esperanza. Salta.

Señor de los Milagros: Diez es la salvación.
¿No me respondes?

TO ANNE FRANK

Lord, make me worthy of this number.
Remember, like yesterday, what burning arrow
passes over the earth.
My cross nails itself wrathfully
into your enigmas.

My sorrow walked naked
through the infertile camp of steel and shrapnel.
I played the violin at Auschwitz,
canto allegro, Ninth Symphony,
Enlightenment that melancholy Beethoven directed
between silenced semitones and deafness.

Treblinka opened my thighs of impiety.
Perhaps I dreamed dramas or invented bitterness
to ingratiate myself with the world?

Not a saint. Nor a heroine.
My naked skin has seen too much
of these wrathful times.
Perhaps the Apocalypse will arrive
when my holy number
is erased before Your eyes?

One hundred eighteen thousand. Fateful number
my forearm displays. Saintly seal.
I soar, I soar filled with my grace. Higher.
Up high. Hope springs up, springs up. Springs up.

God of Miracles: Ten is salvation.
Won't you answer me?

Translated by Roberta Gordenstein

OTRA VEZ, ANA FRANK

Su lenguaje melodioso se enciende
en babeles coloridos.
Abajo, la mar, el cielo que no sabe
el idioma de la sangre.
Ana Frank no ha muerto,
nadie ha muerto, hoy, nadie.
Mi espectro queda allí,
detrás del moisés,
detrás del piano.

Desdoblarse es total,
es permanente,
allí yazgo, vivo en él
cuando el avión conmigo parte.

Ana Frank no ha muerto,
nadie ha muerto, hoy, nadie.

ELINA WECHSLER

ONCE AGAIN, ANNE FRANK

Her melodious tongue lights up
in colorful bedlam.
Below, the sea, the sky that knows not
the language of blood.
Anne Frank has not died,
no one has died, today, no one.
My spectre remains there,
behind the bassinet,
behind the piano.

The act of unfurling oneself is complete,
permanent,
there I lie, I live in him
when the plane with me departs.

Anne Frank has not died,
no one has died, today, no one.

Translated by Darrell Lockhart

EL CEMENTERIO MACABEO EN GUANABACOA

En las afueras de La Habana
están los judíos
que jamás se irán de Cuba
hasta que no llegue
el Mesías.

Allí está la tumba
del padre de Sender Kaplan
la tumba de un rabino
rodeada de un cerquillo de hierro
gozando de la sombra de una palma real.

Allí está la tumba
con sus letras hebreas
que hablan en español
de corazones tristes.
Ay kerida, por qué te fuiste?

Allí está la tumba
con su Estrella de David
toda torcida.
Allí está la tumba
gratinada como un queso feta.

Yo estoy buscando
la tumba de un primo
que era demasiado rico
para morir.

Me desespero.
Le he prometido una foto
a mi tía y mi tío.
Ellos se hicieron hasta más ricos en Miami,
pero no quieren darle ni un centavo a Fidel.

RUTH BEHAR

THE JEWISH CEMETERY IN GUANABACOA

Outside of Havana
are the Jews
who will never leave Cuba
until the coming
of the Messiah.

There is the grave
of Sender Kaplan's father
a rabbi's grave
encircled by an iron gate
shaded by a royal palm.

There is the grave
in Hebrew letters
that speak Spanish
words of love and loss.
Ay kerida, why so soon?

There is the grave
with a crooked
Star of David.
There is the grave
crumbled like feta.

I go searching
for the grave
of my cousin
who was too rich
to die.

I despair.
I've promised a picture
to my aunt and uncle.
They're rich now in Miami
but not a penny for Fidel.

Y de repente la encuentro—
la tumba de Henry Levin
que se murió de leucemia
a los doce años
y no lo pudieron salvar con dinero.

Pobrecito
lo dejaron atrás
con los pocos judíos vivos
y todos los muertos
a quienes las rezan las palomas.

Subo la cámara a mis ojos
y no me deja disparar.
Noventa millas de puentes quemados
he venido viajando
y mi primo no quiere sonreírse.

Tengo que regresar otro día
para llevarme la tumba de Henry Levin
con la cámara de una amiga.
La mía no se recupera en todo el viaje,
queda como una momia, muerta.

Mucho después entiendo
porque Henry Levin
me rechazó a mi
por llegar tarde
a su tumba.

Mi tía y mi tío estaban equivocados.
Su hijo no esta abandonado.
La criada que tuvieron, la mujer negra
que no se casó por estarlo cuidando
no ha dejado de acariciar su tumba.

Tere me dice que ella no se puede olvidar
de Henry porque lo cuidó en sus brazos.
Tu familia allí te dejó, primo,
así que dale gracias a Dios
que una mujer negra visita tus huesitos.

And then I find it—
the grave of Henry Levin
who died of leukemia
at age twelve
and money couldn't save him.

Poor boy,
he got left behind
with the few living Jews
and all the dead ones
for whom the doves pray.

I reach for my camera
but the shutter won't click.
Through ninety long miles
of burned bridges I've come
and my cousin won't smile.

I have to return another day
for Henry Levin's grave
with a friend's camera.
Mine is useless for the rest
of the trip, transfixed, dead.

Only later I learn
why Henry Levin
rejected me
a latecomer
to his grave.

My aunt and uncle were wrong.
Henry Levin is not abandoned.
Your criada, the black woman
who didn't marry to care for him,
tends his grave.

Tere tells me she can't forget
Henry, he lay dying in her arms.
Your family left you, cousin,
so thank God for a black woman
who still visits your little bones.

LOS LIBROS DE LOS MUERTOS

Por eso dedicamos nuestros libros
a los muertos.
Porque tenemos la vana convicción
de que nos escuchan.
Nosotros, cómplices de oficios
menos inocentes,
creemos que seremos dioses
en otros mundos
porque pensamos que la felicidad
es la distancia del milagro
cuando soñamos con una palabra,
cuando vemos alzarse los aviones.

MARTA KORNBLITH

THE BOOKS OF THE DEAD

That is why we dedicate our books
to the dead.
Because we hold the vain belief
that they listen to us.
We, accomplices of less innocent
occupations,
believe we will be gods
in other worlds
because we think that happiness
is the distance from the miracle
when we dream about a word,
when we see airplanes lift off.

Translated by Roberta Gordenstein

LOS PADRES

Tus padres te miran.
Ellos habitan en tus delirios.
Te recuerdan las fechas,
el cumpleaños, el aniversario.
Te corrompen tus sueños.
Conspiran en las viejas fotos.
Te anuncian tu próxima liberación.
Tus padres te dicen:
Todo tiene solución
menos la muerte.
Pero yo sé que nunca más
callarán mis nervios
y me hundiré en mi muerte simbólica.
Sin más definiciones.

PARENTS

Your parents look at you.
They dwell in your deliriums.
They remind you of the dates,
the birthday, the anniversary.
They spoil your dreams for you.
They conspire in the old photos.
They announce your impending liberation to you.
Your parents tell you:
Everything has a solution
except death.
But I know that never more
will they calm my nerves
and I will sink in my symbolic death,
without further definitions.

Translated by Roberta Gordenstein

VERGÜENZA

La precisa documental alemana muestra los horrores de Auschwitz.
La señora polaca sentada a mi lado está callada y calma.
Las imágenes me atacan y empiezo a llorar.
Salgo al hall. Ella me sigue y acaricia mis hombros.
Me dice en su espeso acento:
"No deberías ver esta película. No es buena para ti."
La vergüenza me abruma.
"¿Cómo es posible que seas tú, la que estuviste allí, la que me
  consuele a mí?"
Moviendo su mano, como si espantara a una mosca, me
responde:
"Oh, yo ya estoy acostumbrada...la veo todas las noches..."

MATILDE SALGANICOFF

SHAME

The precise German documentary reveals the horrors of Auschwitz.
The Polish woman seated next to me is quiet and serene.
The images assail me and I begin to cry.
I go out to the hall. She follows me and caresses my shoulders.
In her thick accent she says:
"You shouldn't see this film. It isn't good for you."
Shame oppresses me.
"How is it possible that you, who were there, are
consoling me?"
Moving her hand, as if to frighten off a fly,
she replies:
"Oh, I'm just used to it...I see it every night..."

Translated by Celeste Kostopulos-Cooperman

LUBA I

Tomo
su herencia
de edades en quiebra
los oficios tristes
del abandono
Sus muertos

JACQUELINE GOLDBERG

LUBA I

I take on
her legacy
of bankrupt ages
the sorrowful craft
of abandonment
Her dead ones...

Translated by Joanne Friedman

LUBA II

Luba
diálogo
de pasillos diurnos

Raíz

Memoria que soy

JACQUELINE GOLDBERG

LUBA II

Luba
conversation
along daily corridors

Root

Memory that I am

Translated by Joanne Friedman

LUBA III

No habla
de las primeras ventanas
que desnudó
su fatiga
Para ella
todo es escombro

   Tiempo de elegidos

JACQUELINE GOLDBERG

LUBA III

She does not speak
of the early windows
that undressed
her weariness
In her mind
all is rubble

Time of the chosen

Translated by Joanne Friedman

MI PADRE

No fue sabio
No fue justo
No fue valiente

Sólo un pobre carpintero judío
recorriendo el verano
en bicicleta

Detenido en Tolstoi
entre los cielos de Chagall
hacia la tierra prometida
Jerusalén fue un sueño
que terminó en abandono

No fue músico
No fue rabino
No fue maestro

Sólo un pobre carpintero judío
remontando la guerra
y el origen
para vivir a tiempo
en la palabra de su hija.

MANUELA FINGUERET

MY FATHER

He was not a wise man
He was not a righteous man
He was not a valiant man

Only a poor Jewish carpenter
traveling through summer
on a bicycle

Tarrying over Tolstoy
among the heavens of Chagall
towards the Promised Land
Jerusalem was a dream
that ended in abandonment

He was not a musician
He was not a rabbi
He was not a teacher

Only a poor Jewish carpenter
overcoming the war
and his origin
to live for eternity
through his daughter's words.

Translated by Roberta Gordenstein

LOS TRENES

Siguen. Continúan pasando los trenes.
No tienen cuando acabar los trenes.
Por los rieles de la locura van.
Atraviesan. Cruzan europas humeantes,
bosques afiebrados, aldeas de puertas selladas,
campanarios, noches y basuras. Lentos
puentes. Lutos lentísimos.

Por ahí: se les oye venir,
se les siente venir. Es como un escalofrío
en las patas de los insectos o en el ojo
vivo de un leñador tranquilo, lejos.

Espántanse los estanques. Huyen los venados
con su levedad más pura. Huye el aire.

Pero nadie, nadie sabe—eso dicen—
de dónde vienen, a dónde van, qué es lo que llevan.
Y sin embargo en las estaciones paran,
estiran sus atroces miembros,
descansan las ruedas de la noche.
En las estaciones de párpados melancólicos
se quedan un rato, jadeando.

Algunos paisanos—gente rural y silenciosa--
abren la boca y miran. Muerden un pedazo
de pan duro del invierno, y miran.
Y habrá alguno que, a la partida, agite
su pañuelo blanco analfabeto y hasta sonría;
ése tal vez no sepa nada.

"Madre, cuando sea grande, quiero ser maquinista"
¡Ah, pero nunca, nunca de ese tren! ¡Nunca!
Más te valdría, pequeño, no haber nacido:
no tener manos para cazar relámpagos
en un estanque.

SARINA HELFGOTT

THE TRAINS

They continue. The trains keep on passing.
Endlessly they pass. Along the tracks of madness.
Crossing. They go by smoking European cities,
feverish forests, villages with sealed doors,
bell towers, nights and garbage heaps. Slouching
bridges. Lingering sorrows.

They are coming from over there: one can hear them come,
one can feel them come. Like the twitching
in insect legs or in the sharp eye
of a tranquil woodsman, far away.

The ponds become agitated. The deer flee.
With their lightness of being. The air flees too.

But no one, no one knows—that's what they say—
where they come from, where they are going, what they carry.
But nevertheless they stop at the stations,
stretching their huge limbs,
resting their wheels in the night.
In the stations of melancholy eyelids
they stay awhile, panting.

Some country folk—rural and silent people—
open their mouths and stare. They bite into a hard
chunk of winter bread, and stare.
And at the departure, there will probably be someone
smiling and waving his white, illiterate handkerchief;
he, perhaps, doesn't know anything.

"Mother, when I'm older, I want to be a conductor."
Ah, but never, never of that train! Never!
Little one, it would have been better, had you never been born:
never possessing hands to catch lightning flashes
in the pond

Son tumbas casi estos negros trenes que parten,
que siempre están partiendo o llegando.
Ataúdes sin fin, desmesurados. Ataúdes
al fin y al cabo, con un horario preciso

que si lleva puntualmente
al norte del dolor
al oeste del lamento.

No sé si van o vienen, pero es todo lo mismo.
A Auschwitz, a Belsen, a Dachau,
a los crematorios, a los hoyos
del horror. Se dirigen a las fosas comunes
con el preciado cargo,
con su mundo,
con los que tienen que morir de toda forma.

Las madres detenidas ante el dolor
durante todo el viaje,
los hombres dejando el paisaje
con el sabor a fruta muerta
en sus labios.

They are tombs, almost, these black trains that depart,
that are always leaving or arriving.
Endless, insolent coffins. Coffins,
when all is said and done, with a precise schedule

that is carried out punctually
to the north of pain
to the west of wailing.

I don't know if they are coming or going, but it's all the same.
To Auschwitz, to Belsen, to Dachau,
to the crematoria, to the pits
of horror. They head for the mass graves
with their precious cargo,
with their world,
with the ones who must die anyway.

Mothers arrested by grief
during the whole of the journey,
men leaving the landscape behind
with the taste of death fruit
in their mouths.

Translated by Celeste Kostopulos-Cooperman

A VEINTE AÑOS DE AUSCHWITZ, BERGEN-BELSEN Y LOS OTROS

¿Dónde guardarán el alma los algarrobos,
los pinos o los alerces?
¿Dónde sufrirán a Dios?
¿En qué lugar alguno de triste corazón
buscará el suicidio?

¿Cómo vivirán las estaciones, la enfermedad,
el amor, la locura, la muerte?
¿Con qué lenguaje expresará el silencio
la vejez de los árboles?

¡Cómo hallar vuestra lengua, me digo,
cómo saber de vosotros la verdad
—porque también habéis sido testigos y por tanto cómplices—
cómo sacudir este sopor,
cómo limpiar nuestras raíces,
cómo recibir el sol con esta alma empozada,
con el hierro, la memoria y tanta sangre olvidada
y peligrosamente muerta y viva entre las manos!

LUISA FUTURANSKY

TWENTY YEARS FROM AUSCHWITZ, BERGEN-BELSEN AND OTHER CAMPS

Where will the locust, pine and
larch trees keep their soul?
Where will they experience God?
In what sad-hearted place
will the suicide search?

How will the seasons, illness,
love, madness, death endure?
In what language will silence express
the oldness of the trees?

How will I find your voices, I ask myself,
how will I learn from you the truth
—because you have also been witnesses and so accomplices—
how can we shake off this drowsiness,
how can we cleanse our roots,
how can we receive the sun with our stagnant souls,
with weapons, memories and so much blood forgotten
and dangerously alive and dead between our hands?

Translated by Celeste Kostopulos-Cooperman

LA CASA VACÍA

La casa vacía
llena de acordes
(vivo sin vivir en mí)
y un puro soñar
que se mete en el cuerpo
como intruso misticismo.

Me busco en el amor
vivo con la raíz en la hoguera
      a ella vuelvo
como a una cuenca primera
en la que tiemblan, vencidas, las
sobrevivientes respuestas
crece la tierra que brota dentro de mí
y florecen mis íntimos frutos perplejos.
vino verde de mi estío
          vivo estás.

Casi tan claro
      los fantasmas peregrinos
se acuestan a mi lado   se esconden en los rincones
      se envuelven en la penumbra
         ignorante y breve.
Hay entre cenizas de llanto
un andar confuso
      un día desbocado.

AIDA GELBTRUNK

THE EMPTY HOUSE

The empty house
filled with chords
(I live without living in myself)
and a pure dreaming
that places itself in my body
like instructive mysticism.

I seek myself through love
live with the root in the bonfire
            return to her
as if to a primary river basin
in which the surviving responses
tremble, vanquished
the earth that springs forth inside me grows
and my intimate perplexed fruits flourish,
young wine of my summer
                        you are alive.

Almost as clearly
            the pilgrim phantoms
lie down at my side   hide themselves in the corners
            wrap themselves in the ignorant and brief
                        penumbra.
Among ashes of sobbing there is
a confused gait
                  a broken-edged day.

Translated by Roberta Gordenstein

LO QUE IMPORTA

Lo que importa
ya no importa
si importaba.
Que más para saber
me queda.
De regreso estoy
sin haber ido,
en el mínimo pozo
de este mundo.
Ni vanidad o euforia
quedan o me integran,
o ganas de maldecir
con gestos o con puños:
se me ha ido la fuerza
de mi propia ternura,
y no puedo quererme
ni siquiera a escondidas.
Esto es morir,
quien se anima a negarlo:
repito las mismas miradas
a las cosas,
duermo en pura paz
como las ratas
y me empujo vehemente
a una esquina cercana.
Para vivir detrás
olvido a las parejas
y me gustan los niños
como duendes que alejan
la rigidez del frío.
Ni las pasiones

TERESA PORZECANSKI

WHAT MATTERS

What matters
no longer matters
if it ever mattered.
What else is left
for me to know.
I am back again
in the smallest pit
of this world
without having gone.
Neither vanity nor euphoria
remains or forms me,
nor desires to curse
with gestures or with fists:
the strength of my own tenderness
has left me,
and I cannot love myself,
not even stealthily.
This is dying,
who dares to deny it.
I repeat the same glances
at things,
I sleep in pure peace
like the rats
and I push myself vehemently
into a nearby corner.
In order to live behind
I forget couples
and enjoy the children
like imps who drive away
the rigidity of cold.
Neither passions

ni las divagaciones,
ni los delirios
o sextos y séptimos sentidos,
en mi completo vaciamiento
nada queda:
hueca como estoy
todo retumba
en ecos distorsionados
y perplejos.
Hoy primavera
y tarde de domingo,
la heladera tintinea
sus cubitos:
ya no se trata de soledad
sino de espacio
y de llevar a dormir
a mi cansancio.

nor digressions
nor deliriums
or sixth and seventh senses remain,
nothing,
in my total emptiness;
hollow as I am
everything resounds
in distorted
and perplexed echoes.
Today, spring,
and Sunday afternoon,
the freezer rattles
its little ice cubes:
it is no longer about solitude
but about space
and about carrying off my weariness
to sleep.

Translated by Roberta Gordenstein

LA CASCADA DE LA MUERTE

Vías de plata paralelas
espeso humo que se ladea
rugir de la máquina:
monótono rodar y chirriar.

¿Cúal es el encierro
tras de la madera violada?

¿Quién bate las alas
del pájaro que no vuela?

¿Quién muere de sed de amor?
¿Quién amamanta el vacío de la lágrima?

¿Quién carece de saliva para beber?
¿Quién erige el alimento de los rezos?

Una por una, la muerte en cascada.

El paisaje no visto
(tras de la madera violada).
El aire que no entra.
El agua que no cae.

Al ritmo de las vías de plata
la asfixia de los justos
es sólo el ladrido del perro
que espera junto al guarda.

Alambre de púas: tejido incompleto: vacío encuadrado
Huesos aferrados en el tránsito de la muerte.
Huesos calcinados, tan blancos: puros.
Polvo hecho polvo de estrellas.

ANGELINA MUÑIZ HUBERMAN

CASCADES OF DEATH

Parallel tracks of silver
thick slanted tower of smoke
the roaring of an engine:
monotonous rolling and squeaking.

What is locked up
behind raped wood?

Who will beat the wings
of the bird that cannot fly?

Who dies of thirst for love?
And who will nurse the emptiness of tears?

Who lacks saliva enough to drink?
Who raises up the nurturing of prayer?

Deaths, one by one, cascading down.

Countryside never seen
(beyond raped wood).
Air that cannot enter.
Water that will not fall.

To the rhythm of silver tracks
the asphyxia of the upright
is only the barking of a dog
that waits next to the guard.

Barbed wire, incomplete weaving: framed emptiness.
Bones that hold on tight before the transit to their death.
Incinerated bones, so white: so pure.
Dust made stardust.

Astillas en la piel clavadas.
Desmenuzamiento de la creación.

La ruptura de las vasijas
se desliza hacia al abismo:
la armonía no podrá ser restaurada.
Todos los muertos en el juicio final
serán la única luz que rompa el amanecer.

Despreciable verdugo de la bota negra
no encuentra qué podredumbre pisar
Amasa su propio exorcismo
y su vómito es su deleite.

Uróboro que lame la fuente de sus desechos.

Tal vez un niño se ha salvado:
el cataclismo no será total.

De la fosa de los cadáveres
emerge la nueva piel, el nuevo hueso.

La tierra será fecundada
El fuego se invertirá
El aire esparcirá el olvido
Al agua sólo le quedará lavar perdones

Bajo el peso de los cadáveres
algo bulle, algo germina, algo alienta.

Apartando brazos, piernas y cráneos
un niño al que le brotan
ramas, hojas y frutos
emerge sonriendo de la muerte
que todo redime.

Splinters imbedded in skin.
Shattering of all creation to smithereens.

The breaking of vessels
rolling down the abyss:
harmony could never be restored.
All of the dead in the final judgment
will be the only light
that dawns.

Despicable executioner in black boots
does not find rotten flesh to step on.
He kneads his own exorcism
and his vomit is his delight.

Ouroboros* who licks the source of his own excrement.

Perhaps a child has been saved:
the cataclysm will not be complete.

From the communal grave
the new skin comes, new bones.

The earth is fertilized.
Fire turns around.
Air spreads forgetfulness.
Water will have no job but to wash away pardon.

Under the weight of corpses
something seethes, something germinates,
something breathes.

Making his way amidst arms, legs and skulls,
a child bursting with branches, leaves, fruits,
emerges smiling from the
all-redeeming death.

Nuevas plantas crecieron
nueva sombra de árbol cayó
(lluvia, bendita lluvia)
el campo de los condenados fructificó.

Entre las vías de plata
sola la herrumbre:
ni el eco del perro
ni la bota del verdugo
ni la marcha del soldado.

La nada absoluta.
Los martirizados perduraron

Ola de mar que no se abate

El todo absoluto.

New plants have grown.
New shade of trees fell on the field
(rain, blessed rain).
The field of the damned is in full bloom.

Between the silver tracks
only rust:
neither the echo of a dog
nor the boot of the guard
nor the march of the soldier.

Absolute nothingness.
The martyred ones prevailed:

Wave of the sea that does not yield.

Absolute all.

Translated by Aurora Camacho

*Ouroboros is a mythological serpent who, in eating his own tail, forms a
perfect circle and a metaphor for solipsism and sterility.

FABULAR DE LA PIEDRA

En algún lugar
que es sólo sueño
el infinito descubierto
fábula en la piedra.
La continuidad misma
de la vida.
Los enigmas
los grandes silencios
traen en las sombras
el cansancio
de las luces perdidas
en las estructuras
del tiempo.

JULIA GALEMIRE

INVENTING FABLES ABOUT THE STONE

In some location
that is only a dream
exposed infinity
invents fables about the stone.
The very continuity
of life.
Enigmas
great silences
carry in the shadows
the weariness
of lights lost
in the structures
of time.

Translated by Roberta Gordenstein

LOS ESPEJOS

En el día del entierro
uno anda como un ciego.
En la casa,
nos esperan ansiosos
los espejos.

MARTA KORNBLITH

MIRRORS

On the day of a funeral
you walk like a blind man.
At home,
the mirrors await us
anxiously.

Translated by Roberta Gordenstein

SER INMIGRANTE

Sin audiencia, sin historia.
La memoria no compartida.
La nueva agenda todavía en blanco.

La gente que, amablemente,
pero sin pedir permiso,
rasguña con sus preguntas
las escaras de su soledad.

Respuestas que la dejan,
como una planta desechada,
con las raíces desnudas, ahí, al sol.

MATILDE SALGANICOFF

BEING AN IMMIGRANT

Without an audience or a history.
Unshared memories.
The datebook still blank.

People who kindly
but without asking permission
scratch with their questions
the scabs of her solitude.

Answers that leave her,
like a discarded plant,
with its roots exposed out there in the sun.

Translated by Celeste Kostopulos-Cooperman

JARDÍN DE AUSCHWITZ

Soñé con Auschwitz,
caballos, fogoneros, verdugos y bufones,
        arterias, vapores y calderas.
Soñé toda aquella noche
expediciones al sol con la brújula de Icaro en la piel,
la escalera sin peldaños
es para subir a tomarle medidas al cielo.
El carnaval de antebrazos tendía sus números al viento:
4 56 28 -- 4 56 30, fáciles como cualquier teléfono
salvo que morados e indelebles.
Yeguas finas lo portaban en el trasero
¡A lomo!
a corso
en cuatro patas!
Todos subían a tomarle medidas al cielo:
hadas, marinos, poetas,
oficiantes del sueño y la parroquia
condes, sastres, monjas,
profetas y conversos,
todo suerte de aves y reptiles,
guerilleros, prostitutas.
Todos trepasan aquella gradería.
La muerte caía vertical
mientras ellos se empecinaban en el éxodo.

AUSCHWITZ GARDEN

I dreamed of Auschwitz,
horses, stokers, executioners and buffoons,
        arteries, vapors and cauldrons.
I dreamed all night
of expeditions to the sun with the compass of Icarus
        emblazoned on the skin,
the stepless ladder
for climbing up to measure the sky.
The carnival of forearms flaunted their digits:
4 56 28 -- 4 56 30, easy as phone numbers
but purple and indelible.
Purebred mares wore them on their buttocks,
the post-horse
on its rump,
on all four legs!
Everyone climbed up to measure the sky:
fairies, sailors, poets,
officers of the parish and of sleep,
counts, tailors, nuns, prophets and converts,
every species of fowl and reptile,
guerrillas, whores.
All of them climbed the steps.
Death fell vertically
while they pressed on with their exodus.

Translated by C.D. Wright and Lida Aronne-Amestoy

173

MALETÍN DE VIAJE

En un claro
del bosque,
cercana a los precipicios
de la noche cabizbaja
y la auscencia,
ahí estaba
una pequeña maletita
de niña.
Podría haber sido
como la de tu hija,
llena de gracias,
piedras diminutas
y salvajes,
joyas imaginadas.
Podría haber sido la
valija de la novia
con su vestuario de color malva
como el amor
o la lluvia en el alma
después del amor.

Sin embargo,
era la maleta de una
niña judía
la que cantaba de noche
y que vivió tal vez en Praga,
o Amsterdam,
o en una aldea nevada de Rumania.

Su crimen era haber nacido judía
y nada más.
De pronto, su maleta se halla
entre las nieblas
y el humo azul,
a la deriva.

TRAVELING VALISE

In a clearing
of the forest
near the precipices
of the crestfallen night
and absences,
there was
a small girl's
traveling bag.
It could have been
like that of your daughter,
full of charmes,
small and wild
pebbles,
imagined jewels.
It could have been
the bride's valise
with her mauve clothes
like love
or rain on the soul
after love.

However
it was the bag
of a Jewish girl
who sang at night
and who perhaps lived in Prague,
or Amsterdam,
or a snowy village of Romania.

Her crime was being born Jewish,
nothing more.
Suddenly, her bag is found
between the mist
and blue smoke,
drifting.

No tenía destino
ni dueña y
tan sólo decía
"Auschwitz".

¿Es Auschwitz una ciudad
de muertos o vivos?
preguntó la niña soprendida.

Era una maletita pequeña
con los tesoros de las niñas
y sus delirios de primavera.
Era una maleta sola,
sin destino y
sin dueña.
Esa maletita fue a dar a
un lugar donde al llegar
los niños se llenan
de canas blancas y
ya no miran al cielo.

Más que seguro
en el tiempo del hielo
sin fronteras
algún gendarme nazi
se debió quedar con el botín:
tal vez una muñeca
o un diario,
tal vez semillas de girasol
pero tan sólo un recuerdo.

It had no destination
nor owner and
only said
"Auschwitz."

Is Auschwitz a city
for the dead or the living?,
asked the startled girl.

It was a small bag
with the treasures of girls
and their longings of spring.
It was an abandoned bag,
without destination or
owner.
This little valise ended
in a place where
upon their arrival
children's hair turns white
and they no longer looked at the sky.

It is more than certain
in the age of frost
without borders
some Nazi guard
must have kept the loot:
perhaps a doll
or a diary,
maybe sunflower seeds
but only a memory

Translated by Laura Nakazawa

JARDIM DE SHANAH

Nevoeiro denso
Água viva
Sons arcaicos
Luz e sombra

Violetas recém-abertas
Orvalhadas
Debruçadas em parapeito branco

Flores Minervais
Esmagadas
Sobrenadando nos bastidores
Miraculosamente intactas

Tempo de mudança, transmutação
Dos bastidores ao cenário branco
Expectante

Cabalísticas letras brancas
Mensageiras
Anunciadoras
A luz da Menorah
Chanukah

Óleo cúsmico
Alimento dos primórdios
Humanidade e o eterno retorno
À centelha divina

SARA RIWKA ERLICH

GARDEN OF SHANAH

Thick fog
Vital water
Archaic sounds
Light and shade

Recently opened violets
Bedewed
Bent on white windowsills.

Flowers to Minerva
Now all trodden
Floating in the theater wings
Miraculously untouched

Time transmuting, changing
From the wings to the white scenario
Expectant

Cabalistic white letters
Messengers
Prophets
Under the light of the Menorah
Chanukah

Cosmic oil
Food of our forebearers
Humanity and the eternal return
To the divine spark

Translated by Auristela Xavier with Sara Riwka Erlich

CUANDO ME ROBARON EL NOMBRE

fui una fui cien fui miles
y no fui nadie.
NN era mi rostro despojado
de gesto de mirada de vocal.

Camino mi desnudez numerada
en fila sin ojos sin yo
con ellos sola
desangrando mi alfabeto
por cadenas guturales
por gemidos ciudadanos de un país
sin iniciales.

Párpado y tabique
mi horizonte
todo silencio y eco
todo reja todo noche
todo pared sin espejo
donde copiar una arruga
una mueca un quizás.

Todo punto y aparte.

Hasta que un día
me devolvieron el nombre
y salí a lucirlo por los pasillos
del mundo.
Máscaras encontré
países perfiles adormecidos
lenguas golosas de novedades
absurdo.

Me dejé caminar así
hacia mi ningún lugar
hacia mi nada
por desfiladeros de huellas

NORA STREJILEVICH

WHEN THEY ROBBED ME OF MY NAME

I was one out of a hundred, out of thousands
and I was no one.
Deprived of gesture, gaze and voice
my face was reduced to the letters, NN.

In my numbered nakedness I walk
alone with them draining my alphabet
in eyeless and selfless rows
draining my alphabet
through gutteral chains
through civic wailing of a country
without initials.

Eyelid and partition
my horizon
all silence and echo
all bars   all night
all mirrorless wall
nowhere to copy a wrinkle
a grimace   a perhaps.

All a full stop and a moving on.

Until one day
they gave me back my name
and I went out to display it through the hallways
of the world.
I found masks
countries' drowsy profiles
tongues greedy for news
the absurd.

I let myself walk like this
toward my nowhere
toward my nothingness
through steep paths of

sin rocío
sin poder traducir
mis cicatrices.

¡Ese nombre no es mío!
El mío

era cien era mil era todos
el mío
era cuerpo era vientre era voz
tenía vecinos silbaba
era diurno y nocturno
era un dios.

Se me ha perdido mi nombre!
por las veredas de un mapa
sin esquinas grité
entre puertas acribilladas de miedo.

¡Quiero mi nombre!
mi nombre propio curvo palpitante
¡Que me lo traigan!
envuelto en primaveras
con erre de rayuela
con o de ojalá
con a de aserrín aserrán.

Mi nombre enredadera se enredó
entre sílabas de muerte
DE SA PA RE CI DO
ido
nombre nunca más
mi nombre.

Enajenada de sujeto
no supe conjugarme
no supe recorrer
el abecedario de mis lágrimas.

dewless bones
unable to translate
my scars.

That name is not mine!
Mine

was a hundred   was a thousand   was everyone's
mine
was body   was womb   was voice
had neighbors   whistled
was diurnal and nocturnal
was a god.

I've lost my name!
I shouted along the trails of a
cornerless map
between doors riddled with fear.

I want my name!
my own, curved, throbbing name
Bring it to me!
wrapped in spring
with an *r* for *rayuela*
and an *o* for *ojalá*
and an *a* for *aserrín aserrán*

My curling name got tangled
between death syllables
DI SAP PEAR ED
gone
a name never again
my name.

Alienated from my subject
I didn't know how to conjugate myself
or how to navigate
the *abc*'s of my tears.

Fui ojos revolviendo ayeres
fui manos atrapando jirones
fui pies resbalando
por renglones eléctricos.

No supe pronunciarme.
Fui piel entre discursos
sin saliva sin vestigios
de donde ni por que

ni cuando ni hasta cuando.

No podrás jamás decirlo!
jamás decirte, pensé.

Pero escribirás
escribiré sí
miles de ges de eres de eses
garabatos vicarios
hijos de mi boca
remolinos de deseos
que fueron nombres.

Escribiré
látigos negros para domar
otras salvajes mayúsculas
ahogándome la sangre.
Resistiré resistirás
con nombre y apellido
el descarado lenguaje
del olvido.

I was eyes looking back upon yesterdays
I was hands snatching at rags
I was feet slipping
through electric lines.

I didn't know how to express myself.
I was the skin between
dry and vacuous speeches
without saliva without vestiges
with no why or wherefore

no whensoever or whereupon.

You will never be able to say it!
never speak for yourself, I thought

But you will write
yes, I will write
thousands of *G*'s   of *R*'s   of *S*'s
vicarious scribbles
offspring rising from my mouth
whirlpools of desires
that were once names.

I will inscribe
black whips to tame
other wild capital letters
drowning my blood.
With first and last names
I will resist   you will resist
the brazen language
of oblivion.

NN: No Name
rayuela: hopscotch
ojalá: hope
aserrín aserrán: popular children's nursery rhyme

Translated by Celeste Kostopulos-Cooperman

PASTEUR ESQUINA 86

Un estallido nombra
el instante
de la danza macabra

Temblor
dicen los que oyeron
caminar
la columna de huesos
acompañando
la agonía

Lamentos de un coro
a punto de estallar
el único grito
que no cesa
Aquí estamos!

Fulgor
dicen los que vieron
arrojar
el humo salvaje
mirando
las piedras desnudas

Horror
dicen los que olieron
partículas
que cubren de polvo
agonizando cenizas

Hay una morada
en esa esquina
de polvo, huesos y piedras
con ochenta y seis gritos

86 PASTEUR CORNER

An explosion names
the instant
of the dance of death

Earthquake
say those who heard
walking
the column of bones
accompanying
the agony

Laments from a chorus
about to explode
the only cry
that does not cease
Here we are!

Fire
say those who saw
burst forth
the savage smoke
watching
the naked rocks

Horror
say those who smelled
particles
that cover with dust
agonizing ashes

There is a dwelling
on that corner
of dust, bones and rocks
with eighty-six cries

repitiendo
Aquí estamos!

Y nada podrán erigir allí

que reemplace
el nombre

de cada nombre
que los nombra

repeating
Here we are!

And they will never be able to build anything there

that will replace
the name

of each name
that names them

Translated by Celeste Kostopulos-Cooperman

ALICIA KOZAMEH

FRAGMENTOS DE SALTOS SOBRE EL EXILIO

37

Se absorbe, se percibe, se capta parcialmente. A los costados de la cabeza la luminosidad envuelve. Pero no abarca. La luminosidad. Tan marítima.

39

Mencionaremos. Recordaremos y mencionaremos. Y dejaremos escrito.

47

Presencia. Opuestos. Ausencia. Fuerzas ejerciendo presiones unas contra las otras, y las tormentas: ¿Quién realmente puede decir, puede reconocer, la diferencia entre estar presente y estar ausente? ¿Qué es estar y que es no estar? ¿Quién esta y quien no esta? ¿Qué es haber estado y haber dejado de estar? ¿Qué es haber realmente estado, de cuerpo completo y presente, en la pelea cotidiana, en la busqueda de un detalle, de una idea, de una manera de ir creando un formato de mayor belleza en que fuera posible contener las dimensiones de este mundo? ¿Qué es haber dejado de estar en calidad de lo que se fue, de lo que se hizo? ¿Qué es haber sido parte de las formas y de los contenidos y haber dejado de serlo?

¿Quiénes estaba y quíen ya no está? ¿Quiénes estaban y quiénes ya no están? ¿Cuántos estaban y cuántos ya no están? ¿Donde están los que antes estaban y que de pronto han dejado de estar?

ALICIA KOZAMEH

EXCERPTS FROM *SALTOS SOBRE EL EXILIO*

37

It's aborbed, perceived, partially picked up. The brightness envelops
all around your head. But it doesn't cover everything. The brightness. So maritime.

39

We will mention it. We will remember and mention. And leave it
written.

47

Presence. Opposites. Absence. Forces exercising pressure against
others, and storms: Who can really say, who can recognize the
difference between being present and being absent? What is to be
there and not to be there? Who is there and who isn't? What is it to
have been and to have stopped being? What it is to have really been
there, body whole and present, in the everyday fight, in the search
for a detail, an idea, a way of creating a shape of greater beauty in
which it would be possible to contain the dimensions of this world?
What is it to have stopped being there as what you were, what you
did? What is it to have been part of the forms and contents and to
have stopped being that?

Who was there and who's not there anymore? Who were there who
are not there anymore? How many were there and how many aren't
there anymore? Where are the ones that were there before and who
have suddenly stopped being there?

Translated by David Davis

Jerusalén/Jerusalem

LUISA FUTURANSKY

MÁS CHAGALL QUE CHAGALL

Es cierto; muchas ciudades conservan
nostalgiosas callejas de antiguas juderías
pero nada como Mea Shearim para perderse
embriagada en sus rancios olores,
en la historia de los lugarejos todos,
anónimos y perdidos de la Europa oriental.

Un suburbio que el tiempo voluntariamente olvida
para que uno pueda reconocer que tal vez descienda
de esos levitones lustrosos y sucios,
de esas caras que rehuyen en el sol
de esos pepinos, agrios pescados y cáscaras de naranjas,
de esa puerta estrecha, entreabierta lo suficiente
como para filtrar una barba cana y el sonido de un violín,

de esas trabajadas, regateadas transacciones,
de la copita de licor con que la casamentera
promete encontrarle —formalmente —el marido o la mujer
antes de que sea demasiado tarde,
de esa salmodia que balsea su torso con cierta rítmica iracundia
ante un rollo de papel amorosamente arropado en violento terciopelo,
de esos extraños galerones que ocultan sudorosas cabezas
por donde asoman labradas guedejas rojizas o cenicientas,
de esos hombres que desvían su paso y su mirada al cruzar una mujer,

de estas pálidas, antiguas niñas,
del daguerrotipo vivo de esas jovencitas
que musitan un idioma suspendido, confuso, trasegado y agónico
de todos los lugares donde sus padres y los padres de sus padres
fueron castigados por esa obcecación con que guardan sus vestidos,
cuecen sus dulces, pulen sus diamantes,
repiten sus oraciones y maldiciones
y estoy segura, día tras día
intentan fabricar, secreta, sigilosamente
un golem que mitigue sus pesares.

LUISA FUTURANSKY

MORE CHAGALL THAN CHAGALL

It is true; many cities conserve
nostalgic alleys of ancient Jewries
but none like Mea Shearim in which to lose oneself
intoxicated in its rancid odors,
in the history of all
the anonymous and abandoned villages of eastern Europe.

A suburb that time voluntarily forgets
so that one might recognize that perhaps it descends
from those dirty and lustrous frocks,
from those faces that avoid the sun,
from those cucumbers, pickled fish and orange peels,
from that narrow door, sufficiently ajar
to be able to filter a grey beard and the sound of a violin,

from those toilsome, negotiated transactions,
from the small glass of liquor with which the matchmaker
formally promises to find you a husband or a wife
before it is too late,
from that psalmody that balances its torso with a certain rhythmic
ire
before a roll of paper lovingly draped in violent velvet,
from those strange sheds that conceal sweaty heads
through which appear the cultivated reddish or ashen locks
of those men who divert their step and gaze upon crossing the path
        of a woman,

from those pale complexioned, old-fashioned girls
from the living daguerrotype of those young women
who mutter a suspended, confused, agonizing and jumbled-up language
from all the places where their fathers and the fathers of their fathers
were punished for the stubbornness with which they keep their garments,
boil their sweets, polish their diamonds,
repeat their prayers and curses,
and I am sure, day by day
secretly attempt to fabricate
a golem that will mitigate their sorrows.

Translated by Celeste Kostopulos-Cooperman

JERUSALÉN, SIN FECHA

puerta por puerta
mosaico raíz del mosaico

cráter del desierto

herida
muy vasta
costra
costurón que no cierra
al aire

el aire

desde Zippori
por ejemplo
la piel
del dromedario

y la ruina de los templarios
cuarto esquinas afianzadas
con sarcófagos de mármol veteado
de huesos y sesos
acaso
para despreciar
a los muertos
en los vivos

de oro iluminada
vergel
subyugada
y a tus pies

LUISA FUTURANSKY

JERUSALEM, TIMELESS

door by door
mosaic root of mosaic

desert crater

deep
wound
stitched scab
that doesn't close
in the air

the air

from Zippori
for example
the skin
of the camel

and the temple's ruins
four corners supported
by streaked marble sarcophagi
of bones and brains
perhaps
to scorn
the dead
among the living

illuminated gold
orchard
subdued
at your feet

Translated by Celeste Kostopulos-Cooperman

GÉNESIS (CAP. VII. VERS. 5)

Vinieron, pues, con Noé al arca,
de dos en dos de toda carne en
que había espíritu de vida.

Se sentaron uno frente al otro
y por primera vez se reconocieron.
Comenzaban a caer las primeras gotas
talladas y precisas.
Las simientes hervían con el contacto
y se colmaron los surcos de maravillas anegadas.
Las manadas
sobre los árboles que cubrían sus lamentos
y todo fue otra vez como al comienzo
una línea verde continúa y trasparente
donde el silencio era sonido perecedero.

GENESIS (CHAPTER VII, VERSE 5)

They came, then, with Noah to the ark,
two by two of all flesh in
which there was the spirit of life.

They sat down one in front of the other
and for the first time they recognized each other.
The first drops began to fall
carved and precise.
Semen boiled with the contact
and furrows were filled to the brim with flooded marvels.
The flocks
above the trees that covered their laments
and everything was again as it was in the beginning
a continuous and transparent green line
where silence was the sound doomed to perish.

Translated by Roberta Gordenstein

LEVÍTICO (CAP. XII. VERS. 2-5)

Y dé a luz varón, será inmunda
siete días; ...y si diere a luz hija
será inmunda dos semanas.

Porque el varón será
razón de mi honor y mi miseria
y por tal
pura serás cuando esté en ti.

Más la mujer
Que a ti te ha cuidado
Y de su pecho has bebido la miel
Se inscribirá de sumisión en tus noches
Porque el goce ha de ser
Engendrado y sepultado.

Al varón alabarás
y de la mujer cuidarás sus raíces.

LEVITICUS (CHAPTER XII, VERSE 2-5)

. . .and give birth to a male, she shall be unclean
seven days;. . .and if she gives birth to a female
she shall be unclean two weeks.

Because the male will be
reason for my honor and my misery
and therefore
you will be pure while he is within you.

But the woman
who has cared for you
and from whose breast you have drunk honey
will be inscribed with submission in your nights
because pleasure must be
begotten and buried.

You will praise the male
and you will care for the woman's roots.

Translated by Roberta Gordenstein

SALMOS, (Cap. CXXXVII Vers. 5-6)

Si me olvidare de ti O Jerusalén,
pierda mi diestra su destreza. Mi
lengua se pegue a mi paladar. Si de tí
no me acordare; si no enalteciere a Jerusalén
como preferente asunto de mi alegría.

Si me acordare de ti, O Jerusalén,
sólo en las vigilias de las venganzas prolongadas
en las miradas pedregosas de los que sucumben
mi estertor se haga lento y profundo,
porque entonces, mi recuerdo de ti,
Oh Jerusalén,
será una máscara
para ocultar las razones de mi memoria
y serás preferente asunto de mi agonía.

PSALMS, (Chapter CXXXVII Verse 5-6)

If I forget thee, Oh Jerusalem,
let my right hand forget its cunning. May my tongue
cleave to my palate. If
I do not remember thee; if I do not exalt Jerusalem
as the preferred subject of my joy.

If I remember you, Oh Jerusalem,
only in the vigils of prolonged vengeances
in the stony glances of those who succumb
may my death-rattle become slow and profound,
because then, my memory of you,
Oh Jerusalem,
will be a mask
to hide the reasons of my memory
and you will be the preferred subject of my agony.

Translated by Roberta Gordenstein

JUEGOS A LA HORA DEL DESIERTO

Erial
de cuerpos y becerros
encarnan
a una tribu
lujuria errante
de tierra prometida

Juegos
a la hora del desierto
maná en huecos
piel de pieles
nómade
en el goce
recuerda
a su amado
en la sal de otros brazos.

MANUELA FINGUERET

GAMES AT THE HOUR OF THE DESERT

Wasteland
of bodies and calves
they embody
a tribe
wandering lust
for the promised land

Games
at the hour of the desert
manna in hollows
skin of skins
nomad
in pleasure
recalls
her beloved
in the salt
of other arms

Translated by Roberta Gordenstein

ISRAEL REVISITADO

Aquí los huesos de los gépidos
las polillas engordadas con maderamen
y sebo rancio de templarios
los gatos, salvajes, angurrientos
todos
los hunos
y los otros
ven las estrellas

LUISA FUTURANSKY

ISRAEL REVISITED

Here, the bones of the Geblites
moths fattened on timber
and rancid temple grease
greedy, wild cats
everyone
Huns
and others
see the stars.

Translated by Celeste Kostopulos-Cooperman

JERUSALÉN

Oh pueblo de las cien puertas
por las que regresamos
en tantos sueños equivocados.

La memoria como el maná
susurra en el vientre
el canto de los ausentes

Es un exceso amar lo que fuimos
cuando la mañana es tan bella
y los rostros
extasiados
anuncian
la redención y el movimiento.

MANUELA FINGUERET

JERUSALEM

Oh town of the hundred doors
through which we return
in so many mistaken dreams.

Memory like manna
whispers in the womb
the chant of the absent ones

It is excessive to love what we were
when morning is so beautiful
and enraptured
faces
announce
redemption and movement

Translated by Roberta Gordenstein

EVA EN EL EDÉN

Barro la vereda una y otra vez en las tardes de
        verano,
descalza como las shikses* del barrio.
Mi madre maldice, porque teme una
asimilación temprana.

* Yiddish: jóvenes no judías

EVE IN EDEN

I sweep the sidewalk, over and over again, in the summer
      afternoons,
barefoot like the shikses* in the neighborhood.
My mother curses, because she fears an
early assimilation.

*Yiddish: young non-Jewish girls

Translated by Roberta Gordenstein

SEFARAD

Sefarad, yo soy el que abandono
Triste y herido
dejando tras mi huella
más de un milenio
poético, florido.
Por la alhambra
enrosco tus verbenas
suenan y gimen
de horror las castañuelas
y...en los cánticos de almizcles perfumados
fuego en el alma lloramos los penados.
Los de mi pueblo
gacha cabeza
dolor amurallado
con lento paso
de escarnios perpetrados
por nuestra España, hoy día nos marchamos...
tras nosotros el cántaro, la piedra
la casa, el risco,
el árbol, nuestra tierra
lo que vivimos, lo que soñamos
nuestros amores y risas enlutadas
toda una vida...
Toda una vida...
¿España? ¡Te dejamos!

OLGA WEISZ KLEIN

SEFARAD

Sefarad, it is I who abandons
Sad and wounded
leaving behind my mark of
more than a millennium
of poetry in bloom.
Through the alhambra
I twist your verbenas
which ring and moan
from the horror of the castanets
and...in the canticle of perfumed musks
we convicts cry with fire in our souls.
My people
sentimental
walled pain
with a slow step
from ridicules perpetrated by our Spain
today we leave ...
behind us comes the pitcher and the stone
the house, the cliff,
the tree, our land
what we live, what we dream
our loves and laughter in mourning
an entire life...
An entire life...
Spain? We are leaving you!

Translated by Leslie MacIntosh

JERUSALÉM

Jerusalém criança que renasce a cada dia
Adolescente iluminada e rebelde
Mulher, violentada, odiada, amada sempre
Jerusalém, Mãe viúva, solitária e sofrida
Poeira mística é o bálsamo que cobre
Teu corpo retalhado e revelado
Abrigando e expondo todas as dores, desesperanças, esperanças

"Shalem" do Rei David. Herodiana. Romana. Bizantina
Bíblica e pré-bíblica
Teu solo já não suporta mais corpos sacrificados
Não nasceste para ser cidade-cemitério, cidade-museu
Ruínas reservadas para os olhos de turistas

Difícil pisar em teu solo, tãdolorida pareces
Meu corpo é pesado para teu sensível chão
História da Humanidade

Cruzo e atravesso teus Portões "cujos nomes fazem sonhar"
Subo ao alto de tuas muralhas, escadarias, recantos
Em toda parte, cicatrizes, feridas excavadas
Quem sabe, um dia, talvez, não muito distante
O alento de tuas Pombas
Transformará as balas mortíferas que te atacam
Em leite e mel?

Jerusalém Espírito
As minorias, os que têm fome e sede de justiça
Oram por ti, Jerusalém
A Humanidade necessita de ti
Unicamente em ti poederá ser celebrada
A Grande Festa Universal

Sara Riwka Erlich

JERUSALEM

Jerusalem a child reborn every day
A tear-away teen enlightened and rebellious
A woman, raped, loathed but forever loved
Jerusalem, widowed mother, solitary sufferer.
Mystic dust is the balm that soothes
Your torn and exposed body
Sheltering and unshielding all its pains, hopes and despairs.

Shalem of King David. Herodian. Roman. Byzantine.
Biblical and pre-Biblical
Your soil cannot bear any more broken bodies
You were not born to be a burial city, embalmed museum,
stately ruins reserved for tourists' eyes

How difficult to tread on your sacred soil, too painful,
my body too heavy for your sensitive ground,
history of all humankind

I enter the gateways whose very name makes one dream
I climb to the summit of your walls, your steps and hidden nooks
On every side the scars, the open wounds, the excavations
Perhaps on a day that can't be distant now
The courage of your grey-winged doves
Will transform the deadly bullets that yet assail you
into milk and honey?

Oh spirit of Jerusalem
The outcasts who hunger and thirst for justice
Pray for you, Jerusalem
Humanity needs you
In you alone can we celebrate
The great unending universal festival

Muro das Lamentações
Getsemani
Monte das Oliveiras
Mar da Galileia
Haifa, Beer-Sheba
Jerusalém, Israel

Transcendentes canções nos unem
Nos reencontramos e a despedida foi e é impossível.
Nós sabemos desde aquela madrugada tecida de confidências amarelas
Á beira do deserto.
Testemunhadas ao longe por beduínos e suas prediletas
Poços ocultos e estrelas ao alcance de nossas mãos.

Wall of lamentations
Gethsemane
Mount of the Olives
Sea of Galilee
Haifa, Beer-Sheba
Jerusalem, Israel

Transcendent songs unite us all as one
We meet again and, again, farewell was and is impossible.
This we have known since that dawn woven of yellow confidence
on the edge of the desert
witnessed in the distance by bedouins and their favorites
hidden wells and stars within range of our grasping hands

Translated by Auristela Xavier, Sara Riwka Erlich, and J.M. Deisler

JERUSALÉN, YO SOY EL PEREGRINO

Jerusalén, yo soy el peregrino
el soldado que llora frente al muro
la sangre del caído
la queja del herido.
Soy, todo aquello que nutre nuestro pueblo
su alma, su conciencia y su destino.

Soy aquel que yace en el camino
serpenteante y estrecho de tus calles
soy, el musgo que crece entre tus piedras
que albergaron perennes ¡tanta historia!
y guardaron grabada en la memoria
los salmos de David.
Soy, el grito que emerge de la tierra
el murmullo de un rezo.
El sonido estridente del shofar
las cúpulas doradas de tu suelo
la mezquita de Omar,
cada trozo que forma tu ornamento
y del Galut, nostálgico, lamento, Soy,
Israel! diciendo al universo
con los ojos, brillantes de emoción
que en tu faz, Jerusalén, está la musa
alarido rugiente de ansiedad
que significa tu nombre
¡Libertad!

OLGA WEISZ KLEIN

JERUSALEM, I AM A PILGRIM

Jerusalem, I am a pilgrim
the crying soldier at the wall
the blood of the fallen
the cry of the wounded.
I am that which feeds our people and
your soul, your conscience and your destiny.

I am the one who lies in the road
the slim serpent of your streets
I am the moss which grows between your stones
that perennially shelters so much history
and guards the psalms of David
engraved in memory.
I am the shout of the earth and
the whisper of a prayer.
I am the strident sound of *shofar*
the golden cupulas of your ground
the mosque of Omar,
every piece of your ornament
and of the Galut, nostalgic, I lament that I am
Israel! telling the universe
with my eyes shining from emotion
that in your face, Jerusalem, is the muse
a roaring shriek of worry
that speaks your name
Freedom!

Translated by Leslie MacIntosh

PAULATINAMENTE

Paulatinamente,
el amor nace,
crece en mí.
Al fin estalla,
rebasa los límites de mis manos
mas, inútil fruta madura,
queda en mí.
La soledad vela los fuegos insomnes.

Y así permanezco,
con la constante tristeza del presente,
aguardando un gesto, un llamado.
Oh si fuese capaz
mataría el amor,
las palabras que siguen vibrando,
volvería a la luz.
Pero no,
desde la inquietud de las sombras,
desde la impotencia nacida del todo,
aún espero.

ELVIRA LEVY

GRADUALLY

Gradually,
love is born,
it grows in me.
Finally it explodes,
exceeds the limits of my hands
but, useless ripe fruit,
remains within me.
Loneliness watches over the sleepless fires.

And so I remain,
with the constant sadness of the present,
awaiting a gesture, a summons.
Oh if I were able
I would slay love,
the words which continue vibrating,
I would return to the light.
But no,
from the restlessness of the shadows,
from the impotence born of totality,
still I hope.

Translated by Roberta Gordenstein

DIOS LE DIJO A ABRAHAM

Dios le dijo a Abraham
Vete de tu tierra y de tu patria
y de la casa de tu padre y de tu madre
a la tierra que yo te mostraré
Ya otro le indicó el camino
que tomó la abuela de su madre
repitió el sendero ya aprendido
como la orden de un sueño
marcado en la memoria
que llevan los ríos peregrinos.
Y así el hijo de su hijo
en el vientre de un pájaro rodó
hacia la tierra
tan circular como su destino.
Vuela el Juicio de Dios.
Cada cincuenta años se repite
el viaje sin cuenta
de cada uno en su generación
de cada árbol se poda una rama;
sangra el tronco (que lo nació).
No crecen brotes, sólo viento candente
y un rumor
que los siglos dicen al oído:
"Siempre es lo mismo que hoy."

AIDA GELBTRUNK

GOD SAID TO ABRAHAM

God said to Abraham
Leave your land and your country
and the home of your father and mother
for the land I will show you
Then another showed him the road
his mother's grandmother had taken
he repeated the already-learned path
like the order of a dream
marked in memory
that pilgrim rivers carry.
And so the son of his son
in the womb of a bird rolled
towards the earth
as circular as his destiny.
The Judgment of God flies.
Every fifty years the journey is repeated without realizing it
by everyone in his generation
a branch is pruned from every tree;
the trunk (that gave birth to it) bleeds.
Shoots do not grow, only a white-hot wind
and a rumbling sound
that centuries whisper in your ear:
"It is always the same as today."

Translated by Roberta Gordenstein

TESTIMONIOS

*"Y me dijo: Hijo de hombre revivirán
estos huesos? Y yo respondí: Señor Yavé,
Tú lo sabes."*

—Ezequiel 37: 5

A Ezequiel, el Profeta

*¿Qué ceniza se alza altiva
en el valle de la transfiguración?
¿Qué huesos, qué molicie
ayer sepultos
configuran esqueletos
vivos y anhelantes?*

*Alzan vuelo
con ruedas de mil ojos
sin saber si más allá
sólo hay soledad o asombro.*

*Ya no lloran los cautivos.
En las alas: mil ojos
alimentan sus lágrimas*

Y se levantan de la fosa.

TESTIMONIES

"And he said to me: Son of man,
will these bones live again?
And I answered: Lord God,
Only You can say."

—Ezekiel 37: 5

To Ezekiel, the Prophet

What ash rises up haughtily
in the valley of the transfiguration?
What bones, what softness
buried yesterday
form skeletons
alive and yearning?

They rise up in flight
with wheels of a thousand eyes
not knowing if beyond
there is simply solitude or astonishment.

The captives no longer cry.
On their wings: a thousand eyes
feed their tears.

And they arise from the grave.

Translated by Roberta Gordenstein

JERUSALÉN, UNA COPA DE VÉRTIGO

Las rosas de Jerusalén son complicadas
Los peregrinos desesperan
El camino de las rosas de la verdad
es absoluto.

Y me duele/s tanto.

Luisa Futuransky

JERUSALEM, A WHIRLING GLASS

Jerusalem roses are complicated
The pilgrims despair
The rose-lined road to truth
is absolute.

And you/it hurt(s) me so.

Translated by Celeste Kostopulos-Cooperman

AUTHOR BIOGRAPHIES

Marjorie Agosín is a poet, writer, untiring human rights activist and a descendant of European Jews who escaped the Holocaust and settled in Chile until forced into exile by Pinochet's dictatorship. Her awards include the Letras de Oro Prize, Latina Literature Prize, Jeanneta Rankin Award for Achievement in Human Rights, United Nations Leadership Award for Human Rights, and the Gabriela Mistral medal of Honor for Lifetime Achievement by the Chilean Government. Dr. Agosin is the author or editor of more than 30 titles including *Lluvia en el desierto / Rain in the Desert* (Sherman Asher Publishing), a finalist for the ForeWord Magazine Book of the Year Award 2000.

Diana Anhalt moved to Mexico at the age of eight with parents escaping the United States' McCarthy era. Anhalt has worked in Mexico City as a journalist and translator and has compiled a book of interviews with people who settled in Mexico after McCarthy titled *Fugitives*. Anhalt's poems explore the theme of a bicultural, bilingual experience.

Schlomit Baytelman was born in Israel and moved to Chile at an early age. There, she became a distinguished actress in the theater as well as on television. She is the author of *Refúgios*, a book of poems in which she explores her ancestry as a displaced child. Baytelman lives in Santiago and continues to perform. The poems published here are from *Afula*.

Ruth Behar was born in Cuba and at a very early age moved to Israel and New York, where she grew up in a Sephardic community. Behar became a distinguished anthropologist, essayist, and poet and is the winner of a Gugenheim and a MacArthur Fellowship . Her books include *Translated Woman*, *The Vulnerable Observer,* and *Bridges to Cuba.*

Sara Riwka Erlich is a descendant of Dutch Jews who settled in Recife, Brazil. A psychiatrist of international standing and author of several books on the mental health of adolescents, she is also a poet and the author of a testimonial collection entitled *O tempo de acacias*. Her work explores memory and the representation of it in the lives of marginalized people.

Manuela Fingueret lives in Buenos Aires, Argentina where she was born and established herself as a writer and journalist. She held the positions of Secretary of Media Communications of the Municipality of Buenos Aires, director of the cultural newspaper *Arca del sur,* and artistic and programming director for FM Jai and has been in charge of the Area of Jewish Culture at the General San Martin Cultural Center. Her collections of poetry include *Tumultos contenidos, Heredaras Babel, La piedra es una llaga en el tiempo, Eva y las máscaras* and *Los huecos de tu cuerpo.*Fingueret is currently the director of the cultural publication *Plural.* The poems published here are from *Heredaras Babel.*

Luisa Futuransky, born in Argentina, now resides in Paris where she works as a translator for UNESCO. Futuransky is the author of many books of fiction, essays, and poetry, in which she explores the condition of exile as well as the poetic Jewish tradition. Among her books are *Babel Babel: El nombre de los vientos, La mala hora, Urracas,* and the acclaimed novel *Son Cuentos Chinos.* The poems in this collection are from *La parca enfrente.*

Julia Galemire is considered an outstanding Sephardic poet in both the Askenazi and Sephardic communities of Uruguay. Much of her work explores the themes of mysticism and the Kabbala. Among her books of poetry are *Al sur del aire, La escritura o el sueño,* and *Fabular de la piedra.* Galemire currently resides in Montevideo, Uruguay.

Aida Gelbtrunk, a distinguished Uruguayan poet, novelist, and film critic, was also an important member of the Uruguayan community. Her collections of poetry, including *Aire de familia,* depict the Jewish experience in Uruguay in the 1940s. Gelbtrunk died suddenly in New York City in September 1999.

Gloria Gervitz is considered one of the most important contemporary poets in Mexico as well as being the distinguished translator of such poets as Anna Akhmatova, Rita Dove, and Susan Howe. Gervitz's poetry is deeply rooted in ancient and contemporary Hebrew poetry as well as Jewish themes generally. Her titles include *Shajarit, Yiskor,* and *Migraciones.* The poems published here come from *Shajarit.*

Jacqueline Goldberg, who was born in Venezuela in 1966, has a Masters Degree in Literature from the Universidad de Zulia and is currently a Social Sciences doctoral candidate. She writes frequently for magazines and newspapers and has edited the "Páginas Literarias" of the magazine *Babilonia* as well as several issues of the magazine *Versiones y Diversiones*, published by the Caracas Ateneo. She wrote *Zamuro a miseria*, a play, in 1991 and has two children's poetry collections: *Una señora con sombrero* (1993) and *Mi bella novia voladora* (1994). Among her poetry collections are *Insolaciones en Miami Beach*, *Máscaras de familia*, and *Trastienda* (for which she was a finalist in the Premio Casa Las Américas).

Sarina Helfgott was born in Chiclayo, Peru in 1928. She is an author, poet and playwright. Among her works is book about the Holocaust *El libro de los muertos*. Helfgott lives in Lima, Peru.

Rosita Kalina has numerous publications in Costa Rica, the United States and Israel. Her collections of poetry include *Cruce de niebla* (1981), *Detrás de las palabras* (1983), and *Los signos y el tiempo* (1986), for which she garnered the First National Prize in Poetry in 1987. She has published one book of short stories, *Esa dimensión lejana* (1996), and a book of poetry, *Mi paz guerrera*, awaits completion. Kalina serves as a member of the Board of Directors of the *Editorial Costa Rica*.

Tamara Kamenszain is a distinguished poet and literary critic from Argentina who also has an active career as a journalist. Her literary work has won her a Guggenheim fellowship. Much of her poetry is based on the scriptures and on representations of oral traditions. Her books include *La casa grande*, *De este lado del Mediterraneo*, and *El texto silencioso*, a collection of literary essays.
The poems published here come from *De este lado del Mediterraneo*.

Marta Kornblith was born in Lima, Peru, in 1959. Her entire literary production took place in Venezuela, where she committed suicide in 1997. She had a degree in Social Studies from the Universidad Central de Venezuela and she was one of the founders and a long-standing member of the literary group Eclepsidra. *Oraciones para un dios ausente* was published in 1995.

Alicia Kozameh is an Argentinean novelist and poet who left Argentina during the 1980s as a result of the military dictatorship. She moved to Mexico and then to Los Angeles, where she currently resides. Kozameh's work is mostly concerned with the political tensions in Argentina and the brutality of the dictatorship as well as with the ways in which language changes under authoritarianism. Her testimonial novels as well as her poetry make public the historical events that form the basis of her writings. Among her books are the novels *Pasos bajo el agua* and *Patas de avestruz.*

Elvira Levy was born in Buenos Aires, Argentina, but moved to Spain, first to Barcelona and then to Madrid where she still lives, due to the dirty war and the difficulty for Jews in Argentina. She has published several books of poetry as well as a major essay on the Jews and the discovery of America.

Mónica Mansur was born in Buenos Aires, Argentina, and emigrated with her family to Mexico City, where she still resides. She is a poet, literary critic, and translator, as well as a Professor of Literature at the University of Mexico. Among her books are *Con la vida al hombro*, *Vértigo*, and *Mala memoria.*

Myriam Moscona was born to Bulgarian parents who emigrated to Mexico after World War II. Trained as a visual artist and literary critic, she is considered to be one of Mexico's foremost poets. Her books include *El árbol de los nombres*, *Las Visitantes,* and *Las preguntas de Natalia.*

The poems published here are from *El árbol de los nombres.*

Angelina Muñiz Huberman was born in Spain and emigrated with her parents during the Spanish Civil War to Mexico City, where she currently resides. Her Jewish ancestry can be traced to the Spanish Inquisition and to the Converso Jews who never left the Iberian Peninsula. Her work has been instrumental in the recovery of Sephardic literature as well as in the re-creation of Jewish medieval work. Author of numerous novels and books of poetry and literary criticism, Muñiz Huberman is a prolific and distinguished author. Her work includes *Morada interior*, *Serpientes y escaleras,* and *La morada del aire.* The poems included here are from *Exilio.*

Alejandra Pizarnik's untimely suicide marked the end of a most distinguished literary career. As one of the leaders of the surrealist movement in Latin America, this Argentine poet's work is largely concerned with the themes of the exploration of poetic language and the intensity of metaphorical expressions. Much of her later work centers on death and the drama of existence. Pizarnik is also well known for her prose poetry and fragmentary writings, mostly addressing her existential plights. Among her books are *El árbol de Diana, El deseo de la palabra,* and *Extracción de la piedra de la locura.*

Teresa Porzecanski, anthropologist and award winning writer, was born in Montevideo, Uruguay. Her published collections of stories, essays, novels, and poetry are *El Acertijo y otros cuentos, Historias para mi abuela, Esta manzana roja, Intacto el corazon, Construcciones, Invención de los soles, Ciudad Impune, Una novela erotica, Mesías en Montevideo, La respiración es una fragua, Perfumes de Cartago, La piel del alma, Nupcias en familia y otros cuentos* and *Primeros Cuentos.* She has received many awards, including the MEC, Municipal, Guggenheim, and Bartolomé Hidalgo. Teresa Porzecanski teaches and conducts research at the Facultad de Ciencias Sociales at the Universidad de la República Oriental del Uruguay.

Mercedes Roffé, born in Buenos Aires, Argentina but currently a resident of the United States, has a Ph.D. in Spanish Literature from New York University and has been a Professor of Modern Literature at the University of Buenos Aires. Her work regularly appears in *El Universal* and *Tokonama: Literatura y traducción* has also been published in *Poesía* (Venezuela), *Hiperion* (Barcelona), *Periódico de poesia* (Mexico), *Sitio, Ghandi, Hojas Rojas,* and *Abisinia* (Buenos Aires) and in two periodicals in the United States, *Chain* and *Boundary 2.* Roffe's many collections of poetry include *Poemas 1973–1975, El tapiz de Ferdinand Oziel, Cámara baja, La noche y las palabras, Memorial de agravios o de las cosas que han pasado en esta tierra,* and *Definiciones Mayas.*

Matilde Salganicoff was born in Buenos Aires, Argentina, but left there in 1964 with her husband, Leon, and two children, Alina and Marcos. Once in the United States, Salganicoff obtained her doctorate, already having degrees in Education and Psychology. She worked as a psychologist for years before sharing her thoughts about women, the Holocaust, and other human rights issues through her poetry. Salganicoff defines her Jewishness as "a bond with the Jewish people, a love for words and knowledge, a respect for human rights and nature, and a duty to serve the community at large."
La Refugiada was published in English in a different version in *The American Voice*(The Kentucky Foundation for Women)

Leonor Scliar-Cabral, poet, author, and essayist, was born in Porto Alegre, Rio Grande do Sul (Brazil). She received her Ph.D. in Linguistics from the University of Sao Paulo in Brazil and her post-doctoral degree from the University of Montreal in Canada. She taught at the University of Santa Catarina and is the President of the International Society of Applied Psycholinguistics. Scliar-Cabral's other published works include *Romances e Cançōes Sefarditas* and *Memorias de Sepharad.*

Ana Maria Shúa, a multitalented poet from Buenos Aires, Argentina has worked successfully as an advertising copywriter, journalist, and film script writer. She has published thirty books and has received acclaim throughout her career. Her first book, *El soy y yo*, won two awards. Two of her novels, *Los amores de Laurita* and the award winning *Soy paciente*, have been made into films. Shúa has been married to the same man for twenty-five years and together they have three daughters.

Nora Strejilevich is an Argentine writer in exile whose literary writings have been published in Canada and the United States. She received awards for her testimonials *Una versión de mi misma* and *Sobre-vivencias.* Her novel *Una sola muerte numerosa* won the University of Miami's Letras de Oro prize. Strejilevich is a professor of Literature at Grand Valley State University in Allendale, MI. "Cuando me robaron el nombre" is from *Una sola muerte numerosa.*

Olga Weisz was born in Buenos Aires, Argentina and emigrated to Israel, where she began writing poetry; and then, later, moved to Santiago de Chile, where she teaches Hebrew at the Hebrew Institute of Santiago. Weisz is the author of two books of poetry. The poems published here are from *Jerusalen.*

Elina Wechsler, born in Argentina to Russian parents, left Argentina in 1977 after the disappearance of her younger sister. Trained in psychoanalysis, Wechsler has published numerous articles in that field along with three collections of poetry: *La larga marcha, El fantasma,* and *Mitomanías amorosas.* Her work became well known in Spain after she began writing in exile, exploring the themes of resignation, migration, and the discovery of self.

Index

INDEX OF TRANSLATORS

Desde GÉNESIS

II
Por la noche,
en este desierto
de Biblias invisibles,
de nómadas y conjuros,
las estrellas nos
cubren
como un libro de rezos.

VI
No hay países entre tú y yo.
No hay espacios ajenos.
No escogemos idiomas.
No hay idiomas para
dividirnos.
Tus amigos ya son los míos.
Untamos la boca como
quienes untan el pan o los
trozos de la memoria
que son una sábana grandiosa
y magnífica que nos
protege
del temor a la paz.

MARJORIE AGOSÍN

From GENESIS

II
Through the night
in this desert
of invisible Bibles,
of nomads and incantations,
stars
spread over us
like a book of prayers.

VI
There are no countries between you and me.
There are no foreign spaces.
We choose no languages.
No language
can divide us.
Your friends are already mine.
We smear our mouths like
those who butter bread or
fragments of memory
that splendid and
magnificent bedsheet that
protects us
from the fear of peace.

translated by Alvaro Cardona Hine

A NOTE ABOUT THE BOOK

This book represents a dance between the languages—English, Spanish, Portuguese, Slavic, Hebrew, Yiddish, Ladino—and the shift between hemispheres as seen in the transposition of seasons in Leonor Scliar-Cabral's poem "Fogo y cinzas / Fire and Embers". Words such as Cabala / Kabbalah and querida / kerida have multiple correct spellings or transliterations, and we have followed the individual author / translator's lead in these dances. Many obstacles arose while tracking down the spelling of names and final revisions of work. We apologize for any remaining missteps.

The book is set in Berkeley Book.

ABOUT THE COVER ARTIST

Liliana Wilson Grez is a Chilean-born painter and graphic artist who currently lives and works in San Francisco. She has exhibited her work throughout the United States and in Italy. Her original painting in acrylics titled *La Llegada* is the cover image for *Miriam's Daughters*. She writes "As a Latin American woman who has lived through a dictatorship in Chile, I use art to give meaning to a life that is at once hard to confront and important to remember."

ABOUT THE PRESS

Sherman Asher Publishing, an independent press established in 1994, is dedicated to changing the world one book at a time. We are committed to the power of truth and the craft of language expressed by publishing fine poetry, memoir, books on writing and other books we love. You can play a role. Bring the gift of poetry into your life and the lives of others. Attend readings, teach classes, work for literacy, support your local bookstore, and buy poetry.